SUMMER SOAK

A Summer Devotional on the Attributes of God

SUSAN L. CADY

DEDICATION

JENNIFER, ZACHARY, AND JACOB

I have no greater joy than to hear that my children are walking in the truth. —
3 John 1:4

ACKNOWLEDGEMENTS

I am grateful to so many whose encouragement and efforts made this project a reality. My mother, Suella Jones, is my biggest cheerleader and encourager. Her own writing inspires me. The editorial and design assistance of Jennifer Byars, Pam Stewart, Tracey Drake, and Haley Sprouse have been invaluable. My husband, Chris, the man with whom I am blessed to walk through life, supports and encourages me in everything I do to share Jesus and God's Word with others.

TABLE OF CONTENT

INTRODUCTION

Summer is the season in which we find ourselves looking forward to a little relaxation! It is time for flip flops and pool parties, longer days of sunlight, basking in the sunshine, and sitting on the porch swing sipping lemonade. It is walking barefoot on a sandy beach, inhaling that fresh salt air, and feeling the caress of warm ocean breezes. It is enjoying ice cream on a hot day and heading outdoors for baseball games, cook outs, and picnics. We look forward to that much-needed and anticipated vacation. It is a season of rest and relaxation before our year cranks back up with a calendar full of activities and demands on our schedules that can just drain us!

During the lazy days of summer, it can be easy to allow our walk with Christ and time in God's Word to take a back seat. This devotional book is designed to give us daily reminders to SOAK in God's Word as we focus upon the character and nature of our glorious God! Psalm 113:3 reminds us to praise the name of the Lord from the rising of the sun to its setting.

From the rising of the sun to its setting, the name of the LORD is to be praised! —Psalm 113:3

One of the greatest benefits of my walk of faith has been to study the attributes and names of God. God reveals Himself to us throughout the Scriptures so that we might know Him and experience the joy found in a relationship with Him. Years ago through a Precept® Bible study, I was taught to mark and note any reference to a name or characteristic of God when reading Scripture. This has been an amazing practice in my life. In times of need, or when I find it difficult to trust God in a particular circumstance, knowing who He is and calling to mind His names and attributes has grown my faith. It transforms my thoughts, attitudes, and actions. The more I know God, the more I love Him, and trust Him in even deeper ways.

We are able to know God because He has chosen to make Himself known to us. God reveals Himself to us and answers our question of 'who is God?' by revealing His character and nature (attributes) to us. An attribute is something that is true of God. God makes Himself known to us through His creation, His Word, His Son Jesus, and His Spirit living in us as believers.

In His Word God reveals Himself and describes His character through His names. We first see Him as Elohim, *Creator God,* in Genesis. Then God makes Himself known to Abraham as *God Almighty.* But in Exodus God reveals Himself by the name that had not been previously known, *I AM that I AM– Jehovah*, which means *to be, to exist, the self-existent one, all sufficient one.* It is the name that denotes the One who makes Himself known unceasingly! It is considered God's most holy and revered name. It is His covenant name. Moses spent time in God's presence, in intimate relationship with Him, and he was forever changed. We can be too!

God is constantly making Himself known to us. We were created for His presence and glory. We were created for fellowship with Him. The infinite, incomprehensible, indescribable, holy God desires to be intimate with us! Pause for a moment and really allow that to sink in.

Not only is *Jehovah* God's covenant name, but His covenantal promise is fulfilled in Jesus. God made Himself known to us in a more intimate way by restoring us into a right relationship with Himself through Jesus. God, *the great I AM*, becomes flesh and we have life!

In the beginning was the word, and the word was with God, and the Word was God. He was in the beginning with God. All things were made through him, and without him was not anything made that was made. In him was life, and the life was the light of men. The light shines in the darkness, and the darkness has not overcome it...And the word became flesh and dwelt among us, and we have seen his glory, glory as of the only Son from the Father, full of grace and truth. —John 1:1-5, 14

Jesus said to him, 'I am the way, and the truth, and the life. No one comes to the Father except through me.' —John 14:6

In him we live and move and have our being... —Acts 17:28

Jesus meets us right where we are—regardless of where we find ourselves. Only He can meet our deepest needs. Only He knows our deepest hurts and disappointments. Only He can satisfy our desires and longings. Only He can give us the peace, joy, purpose, and contentment that we so desperately seek in life. Only He because He IS—Jehovah, the great I AM, the one who WAS, who IS and who IS to COME!

Oh, the depth of the riches and wisdom and knowledge of God! How unsearchable are his judgments and how inscrutable his ways! For who has known the mind of the Lord, or who has been his counselor? Or who has given a gift to him that he might be repaid? For from him and through him and to him are all things. To him be glory forever. Amen.
—Romans 11:33-36

As we go about our busy lives it is easy to lose sight of this glorious revelation! We need to be reminded on a daily basis of who God is and what He has done. Our response to all God has done and the life-giving news of the gospel should be a life characterized by praise and thanksgiving!

Here's a definition for the word *SOAK:*
- to enjoy something
- to use all of something
- to saturate
- to penetrate or affect the mind or feelings
- to fill thoroughly
- to absorb or take in
- to spend time experiencing and enjoying the mood or feeling in a place

The Plan
Each week we'll focus on an attribute of God found in the Word and spend time praising Him. The daily verse or passage of Scripture will teach us something about our weekly attribute of God. Each of these attributes are tied to the imagery of summer—so as we go about our "days of summer", we'll have a visible reminder to focus on who God is!

As we *soak* in God's Word and His presence, we walk away refreshed, renewed, and better prepared to serve others with the love of Christ. The Word refreshes and renews us so we are ready to pour out again.

In our guiding verse for this series, Psalm 113:3, the word *praised* in the original language (Hebrew) is the word, *hâlal*, which means *to be clear, to shine, to make a show, to boast, to rave, to celebrate; to be worthy of praise.*

Praise is the result of contemplating the character and nature of God, and then declaring to yourself and others who God is and what He has done. Let's do just that! Let's allow the imagery we encounter during our summer days to stir us to praise God—*to shine, to boast, rave and celebrate* God's presence in our lives! Just like that sun-kissed glow we radiate after basking in the summer sun, soaking in God's Word and His presence leaves us with a radiance that SHINES as we praise God and reflect Christ to those around us.

The approach for each day's lesson will be to:
- Read the Word.
- Reflect on who God is and what He has done.
- Pray the Word back to the Lord and spend time praising Him.
- Meditate upon His attribute and truth as you go through the day.
- Be still and bask in the warmth of God's presence.
- Shine by sharing and serving others out of the overflow of God's presence and Word in your heart.

It is my prayer that through this series *from the rising of the sun to its setting* we will focus on our amazing God. We'll take that Word for each day and think about it, talk about it, pray it, and share it. We'll allow it to really SOAK into our hearts and lives.

RESOURCES

Throughout this devotional you will find references to definitions for words from Scripture in the original language. In my study of the Scriptures, I use the following Bible reference books:

The Complete Word Study Dictionary: Old Testament, Dr. Warren Baker, Dr. Eugene Carpenter, AMG Publishers; 1st Printing edition (October 1, 2003).

The Complete Word Study Dictionary: New Testament, Dr. Spiros Zodhiates, AMG Publishers; Reissue edition (August 1, 1992).

The Complete Word Study: Old Testament, Dr. Warren Baker, Dr. Spiros Zodhiates, AMG Publishers; 1st Printing edition (June 1, 1994).

The Complete Word Study: New Testament, Dr. Spiros Zodhiates, AMG Publishers; Reissue edition (June 1, 1991).

Strong's Exhaustive Concordance to the Bible, James Strong, Hendrickson Publishing (January 1, 2009).

Week 1

Sunshine and Light

Summer days beckon us outdoors to soak up those warm and relaxing rays of sunshine. Whether you find yourself in the backyard, at the park, poolside, at the beach or driving to work with the sun streaming in your car windows, allow the sunshine and light to move you to praise the Lord.

Day 1 — God is Marvelous Light

SOAK
The Lord is God, and he has made his light to shine upon us.
—Psalm 118:27

God is light and Jesus is the Light of the World!

In the beginning was the Word, and the Word was with God, and the Word was God. He was in the beginning with God. All things were made through him, and without him was not anything made that was made. In him was life, and the life was the light of men. The light shines in the darkness, and the darkness has not overcome it. —John 1:1-5

Sunlight provides the warmth on a summer day that envelops and relaxes us. It is comforting. We just want to sit and soak it up, to relax in its brightness, warmth, and beauty. It leaves us with a radiant glow.

Light is used to shine in dark places where we can't see, to illuminate and reveal the problem so a solution can be derived. Think about it...a plumber looks under your sink for that leak, the doctor shines his pencil light down your throat to expose the infection, the bug man uses a flashlight in corners and dark spaces to see where bugs might have made a home, the light on the end of your vacuum cleaner exposes those places where the dirt and dust have come to rest, a flashlight illuminates your path and keeps you from stumbling, a nightlight brings comfort when you're fearful...you get the idea.

Light reveals what's hidden in the darkness. In Scripture darkness is associated with sin. Once something is exposed it can be diagnosed, treated, healed, or corrected. This is what the Word of God does to our hearts and lives. It exposes those places that are infested and infected with sin. We often fear and avoid the pain of the exposure but in the end it is always restorative and renewing.

Would you be willing to soak up some light and bask in God's Word allowing it to expose, correct, and heal your heart, soul, and mind? To *bask* means *to lie or relax happily in a bright, warm place; to take pleasure or derive enjoyment.*

We have nothing to fear because God is light. Therefore we can trust and rest in Him—knowing that He loves and cares for us. He sent His Son, Jesus, as the light of the world shining and revealing to us the character and nature of God, providing forgiveness for our sins, and restoring us into a right relationship with Him.

Again Jesus spoke to them, saying, 'I am the light of the world. Whoever follows me will not walk in darkness, but will have the light of life.' —John 8:12

Scripture tells us that we have been called out of darkness into His marvelous light!

But you are a chosen race, a royal priesthood, a holy nation, a people for his own possession, that you may proclaim the excellencies of him who called you out of darkness into his marvelous light. —1 Peter 2:9

SHINE
Reflect on the verses from today and on the fact that God is light! Think about what it means in your life to know that God is light. How does this comfort and encourage you today? Are there areas of your heart and life that are hidden in darkness and need the light of God's Word to heal and restore?

Day 2 — God is Radiant Light!

SOAK

Those who look to him are radiant, and their faces shall never be ashamed. —Psalm 34:5

Yesterday we looked at the fact that light illuminates and is radiant. When we soak up its rays, we are left with a radiant glow. I love to walk along the beach at sunrise or sunset. Seeing the light of the sun reflecting off the water is so beautiful and peaceful. Let's focus on the radiance of God's presence today. The word *radiant* in our verse means *to sparkle, shine, beam, to be cheerful.* It describes a person glowing, beaming, radiant and overjoyed about something. It means to shine, to glow, to beam over deliverance from God.

Those who look to the Lord are radiant. We sparkle, shine and glow as a result of being in the light of His presence. We find complete and amazing joy in our relationship with Him!

What does it mean to "look" to the Lord? In our verse, the word *look* means *to be intensely focused or to gaze upon something, to look to something for help or be dependent upon.* When I look to the Lord, I acknowledge my need for and dependence upon Him in my life. In the light of Jesus' presence, I never need to be ashamed because He has provided the forgiveness for my sins and restored my relationship with God. When I look to the Lord, I evaluate or consider my life and all He has done to restore my joy and peace and to give me hope. This gives me reason to rejoice in Him!

*Long ago, at many times and in many ways, God spoke to our fathers by the prophets, but in these last days he has spoken to us by his Son, whom he appointed the heir of all things, through whom also he created the world. **He is the radiance of the glory of God** and the exact imprint of his nature, and he upholds the universe by the word of his power. After* *making purification for sins, he sat down at the right hand of the Majesty on high.* —Hebrews 1:1-4, emphasis added

... giving thanks to the Father, who has enabled you to share in the saints' inheritance in the light. He has rescued us from the domain of darkness and transferred us into the kingdom of the Son He loves. We have redemption, the forgiveness of sins, in Him —Colossians 1:12–14 (HCSB)

Is there something you are carrying around from your past or present that you need to lay at the feet of Jesus and receive His forgiveness?
Nothing is too great that He cannot cover it. I know! I spent many years walking in shame over things from my past and missing out on the joy and radiance of God's presence. Somehow in my head and heart I felt my sin was too great. But God's love is greater. He sent His Son as living proof of His abundant grace, unfailing love for us, and His power to forgive, heal, and restore us.

Restore us, O God; let your face shine, that we may be saved. Restore us, O LORD God of hosts! Let your face shine, that we may be saved. — Psalm 80:3, 19

Is there sin in your life that is veiling the light of Jesus' presence in your life?

Sin is darkness and therefore always blocks the light.

Is there a situation in your life where you need to look to the Lord for His guidance and direction and to gain some perspective?

SHINE
Reflect on the verses from today and on the fact that God is light! Ask the Lord to reveal anything that is hindering your walk and blocking the light. Confess any sin He illuminates in your heart and walk in the freedom of forgiveness with a radiant face! View your circumstance or situation by gazing upon and contemplating who God is and what He has done for you. As you soak up the sun's rays today in the outdoors, let it remind you that God is light and when we look to Him we are radiant!

Day 3 — God is a Light for My Path

SOAK

Blessed are those who have learned to acclaim you, who walk in the light of your presence, Lord. —Psalm 89:15 (NIV)

Happy are the people who know the joyful shout; Yahweh, they walk in the light of Your presence. —Psalm 89:15 (HCSB)

How happy are those who have learned how to praise You; those who journey through life by the light of Your face. —Psalm 89:15 (The Voice)

Walk – *to go, to walk; metaphorically it is used to speak of the pathways (behavior) of one's life or one's manner of life.*

When we walk in the light of God's presence we are walking in a manner that is pleasing and honoring to Him—and this brings joy to our lives. God's Word is light and God's Spirit illuminates making known to us the truths of His Word. If we want to know more of God and His ways we must be in His Word. The more we know Him the more we trust Him and praise Him for who He is! This gives us reason to be joyful. I love how the HCSB translates *praise* as the *joyful shout*! We come to know through experience the *joyful shout* that results from a life that has meaning and purpose in Christ. We know the *joyful shout* of the gospel and its transforming work in our lives. And this changes our daily walk!

Your word is a lamp to my feet and a light to my path. —Psalm 119:105

The unfolding of your words gives light; it imparts understanding to the simple. —Psalm 119:130

Make your face shine upon your servant, and teach me your statutes. —Psalm 119:135

You have made known to me the paths of life; you will make me full of gladness with your presence. —Acts 2:28

Read Psalm 19.

SHINE

Reflect on the verses from today and on the fact that God is Light! Pray some of the characteristics of the Word you found in Psalm 19. Ask the Lord to reveal anything that is hindering your walk and blocking the Light. Confess any sin the Holy Spirit illuminates in your heart and walk in the freedom of forgiveness with a radiant face! View your circumstance or situation by gazing upon and contemplating who God is and what He has done for you.

As you soak up the sun's rays today in the outdoors, let them remind you that God is light and when you look to Him, you are radiant! Praise and thank God that He has not left you in darkness but has revealed Himself to you through His creation and His Word!

Day 4 — The Lord is My Light

SOAK

The Lord is my light and my salvation; whom shall I fear? The Lord is the stronghold of my life; of whom shall I be afraid? —Psalm 27:1

Just as that nightlight helped to alleviate your fears as a child, the fact that God is light in your life can bring peace in the midst of your fearful times. When we walk in the light of His presence, we experience peace and comfort. There is nothing that can separate us from God's presence in Christ Jesus! We can rest secure in Him.

"Peace I leave with you. My peace I give to you. I do not give to you as the world gives. Your heart must not be troubled or fearful. —John 14:27 (HCSB)

For I am persuaded that not even death or life, angels or rulers, things present or things to come, hostile powers, height or depth, or any other created thing will have the power to separate us from the love of God that is in Christ Jesus our Lord. —Romans 8:38-39 (HCSB)

What are you fearing today? Are you feeling alone and abandoned? Are you unsure of your future? Feeling anxious? Rest secure in the knowledge that your Creator loves you! He will never leave you nor forsake you. Jesus is your peace, security, and hope. He is near. He is Immanuel, God with us!

SHINE
Because the Lord is your stronghold, you have no need to fear. Lay your fears at the feet of Jesus and rise and walk in peace. Praise Him today! (Numbers 6:24-26)

Day 5 — God is Steadfast Light!

SOAK

Every good gift and every perfect gift is from above, coming down from the Father of lights with whom there is no variation or shadow due to change. —James 1:17

We live in a world where there is constant change. New versions, new models, new updates and new technologies are constantly before us. We experience change in relationships, work, the economy, and the list goes on and on. There are times when I appreciate change, like when I redecorate a room in my home. However, I'm not always as accepting and embracing of change in my life.

It comforts me to know that God does not change! When my world is shaking, He is steadfast! He is the God who is the same yesterday, today and forever! I can rely upon and trust Him because He will never leave nor forsake me. When I'm overwhelmed and unsure about the changes in my life, I can look to the One who is steadfast light!

Is there change happening in your life?

Perhaps the changes are exciting, filled with possibilities and anticipation. Perhaps the changes are rocking your world and not what you expected, desired or anticipated.

When change is hard and life is difficult, it is easy to question God and ask *why*. We can rest confidently in the fact that God is not surprised by our questions and difficulty in comprehending. He is infinite, sovereign and all-knowing. He beckons us to cry out to Him and to pour our hearts out to Him! He is our refuge (Ps 62:8). This is one reason knowing the character and nature of our God is so important. We can trust and rest in who God is, even in the midst of not understanding why! He fulfills what He promises in His timing. His presence is steadfast light shining in a dark and difficult world.

Read Psalm 136.
This is a brief history of God's working His plan, in His timing, among His people Israel. The Israelites often grumbled, complained, questioned and doubted God. But those who remained steadfast, trusting Him, and taking Him at His Word, experienced the Promised Land and inheritance. Even though we have not experienced entering the Promised Land with the Israelites or their inheritance of the land, what God promised long ago has been accomplished. We are the recipients of that promise in Christ Jesus! He has given us redemption, forgiveness, new and eternal life. We can trust Him, even when we don't understand it all.

Did you notice the response in Psalm 136?
"Give thanks...His steadfast love endures forever."

What would be your Psalm 136?
Consider writing out your story, and when you're tempted to doubt, grumble, and complain, remember His love endures forever! Give thanks. Give thanks to the Lord, knowing He is working in your life and that He does not change. Rest in His steadfast love and abundant grace. He is steadfast light.

The steadfast love of the Lord never ceases; his mercies never come to an end; they are new every morning; great is your faithfulness. The Lord is my portion, says my soul, therefore I will hope in him. —Lamentations 3:22-24

SHINE
Reflect on the verses from today and on the fact that God is a steadfast light shining in a dark and difficult world. He is faithful and unchanging and you can rest in Him.

6

Day 6 — The Light of the World

SOAK

You are the light of the world. A city set on a hill cannot be hidden. Nor do people light a lamp and put it under a basket, but on a stand, and it gives light to all in the house. In the same way, let your light shine before others, so that they may see your good works and give glory to your Father who is in heaven. —Matthew 5:14-16

Because Jesus is the Light of the World and He has come to redeem us from darkness and sin, we are called to live as light in a dark world. We are to reflect the transforming work of the gospel in our lives. We are to be shining bright lights in a dark world, pointing others to Jesus and bringing glory to God.

What gifts, talents and abilities has the Lord given you? Are you using them to shine brightly for Jesus and reflect His love and grace to those around you?

Do everything without complaining and arguing, so that no one can criticize you. Live clean, innocent lives as children of God, shining like bright lights in a world full of crooked and perverse people. —Philippians 2:14-15 (NLT)

Walk as children of light. —Ephesians 5:8b

SHINE

How does the fact that your daily walk is to be a reflection of how Jesus changes your attitude and actions today? Let your light shine. Reflect on the verses from today and on the fact that God is light. Because you are His child, you are called to be light to a world in need.

Day 7 — God is Everlasting Light!

SOAK

The sun shall be no more your light by day, nor for brightness shall the moon give you light; but the LORD will be your everlasting light, and your God will be your glory. — Isaiah 60:19-20

Soaking up that summer sunshine is wonderful! I hope the sunshine this week has prompted you to praise God for who He is and all He has done in your life. As we close our week of reflection on the fact that God is Light today's verse reminds us that one day, if we know Jesus, we will no longer need the light of the sun, moon, or man-made electricity to provide illumination. The glory of the Lord will be our light and shine brilliantly around us!

Fight the good fight for the faith; take hold of eternal life that you were called to and have made a good confession about in the presence of many witnesses. In the presence of God, who gives life to all, and of Christ Jesus...I charge you to keep the command without fault or failure until the appearing of our Lord Jesus Christ. God will bring this about in His own time. He is the blessed and only Sovereign, the King of kings, and the Lord of lords, the only One who has immortality, dwelling in unapproachable light; no one has seen or can see Him, to Him be honor and eternal might. Amen. —1 Timothy 6:12-16 (HCSB)

SHINE

Reflect on the verses from today and on the fact that God is Everlasting Light! As you step out into the sunshine today be reminded of Jesus, the Everlasting Light shining bright in a dark world.

13

Week 2

Ocean Waves and Mountain Peaks

What is your favorite summer vacation destination? As we plan that much-anticipated trip to the beach, we can almost smell the salt from the ocean waves and feel the soft sand and beneath our feet. The rest we have come to these places to find is reflected in the beautiful sunsets that bring each day to a close. Or we may prefer the cool woodsy smell as we sit on the porch of a cabin tucked into the side of a mountain. We feel the stress fade as we retreat from the noise and busyness of our daily life and refresh ourselves with the quiet that surrounds the beauty of God's creation.

Summertime usually invokes thoughts of the beach, ocean and mountains for many of us—those annual trips to the beach or to the cabin tucked away in the mountains. The imagery of the ocean and mountains make me think of God's power and might. Perhaps your summer will not include trips to any of these destinations this year. But you can join me this week on a mental trip to these places as we focus on the attribute of God's power and might.

Day 8 —He is With Us!

SOAK
*I am the LORD your God, who stirs up the sea so that its waves roar— the Lord of hosts is his name. —*Isaiah 51:15 (ESV)

*The LORD of hosts is with us. —*Psalm 46:7a (ESV)

*The LORD All-Powerful is with us. —*Psalm 46:7a (CEV)

*The LORD Almighty is with us. —*Psalm 46:7a (NIV)

Read Psalm 46.

Life often feels like a battle, whether it be physical, mental, emotional or spiritual. Psalm 46 gives us some powerful imagery—the earth giving way, mountains carried into the midst of the sea, waters roaring and foaming, mountains trembling, nations raging and kingdoms tottering. But we can take comfort and courage in the fact that our God is over all. He is the Lord of Hosts, All-Powerful, Almighty—and in the midst of it all He is with us!

In Isaiah 51:15 and Psalm 46:7 we find the name of God, *Jehovah Sabaoth,* meaning the *Lord of Hosts.* It is the name of God that conveys His power and His omnipotence.

Psalm 46:10 encourages us to be still and know that He IS God!

Be still *– to relax, sink down, let drop, to be quiet.*

Know *– to know, consider, confess, to experience.*

In other words, consider how mighty God is and cease being discouraged and disheartened. Relax, get quiet, and know—*consider, perceive, and experience*—the power of God's presence. Know that He is the all-powerful One who controls the roaring, shaking, raging, and tottering. The Lord of Hosts is fighting for us. The Lord of Hosts is with us! He is our refuge and our strength, a very present help in trouble. When my heart and flesh are failing, He is my strength and my portion (Psalm 73:26).

When you go out to war against your enemies, and see horses and chariots and an army larger than your own, you shall not be afraid of them, for the LORD your God is with you, who brought you up out of the land of Egypt. And when you draw near to the battle, the priest shall come forward and speak to the people and shall say to them, 'Hear, O Israel, today you are drawing near for battle against your enemies: let not your heart faint. Do not fear or panic or be in dread of them, for the Lord your God is he who goes with you to fight for you against your enemies, to give you the victory. —Deuteronomy 20:1-4

Thus says the LORD, who gives the sun for light by day and the fixed order of the moon and the stars for light by night, who stirs up the sea so that its waves roar—the LORD of hosts is his name... —Jeremiah 31:35

Read 2 Chronicles 19:4-20:30. When I find myself in the midst of a battle this is one of my favorite stories to read in Scripture. As you read through these verses take note of what King Jehoshaphat does and does not do, how God works, the outcome of the battle, and the people's response. You will be encouraged, my friend!

SHINE
Reflect on the verses from today and on the fact that God is the Lord of Hosts, Almighty, All-Powerful and Sovereign over all the earth.

Day 9 — Who? Can You?

SOAK
Do you feel as if you need to have it all together and have all the answers? Do you need to control life's circumstances and the people around you? Or perhaps you struggle with feeling as if you are never enough. Read on, sweet friend, today's Scripture passage is for you.

Read Job 38:1-21.

What a humbling passage of Scripture! It certainly puts things into perspective for me. I'm naturally self-focused and self-centered, and therefore tend to make life all about me. I'm like that "proud wave" described in Job 38, rushing the shore and acting as if I can control all things.

When I do this, I lose sight of who God really is. It is humbling to realize how small and insignificant I am compared to Almighty God. It is in this realization that I find myself responding like Job: *I am so insignificant. How can I answer You? I place my hand over my mouth. I have spoken once, and I will not reply; twice, but now I can add nothing.*
—Job 40:3-5, HCSB

But it is when I see God for who He is that life begins to make sense. I gain true perspective, and find comfort, encouragement, freedom, and hope. I know what life looks like when I am left to my own devices, and it is not pretty or productive. I need Jesus every moment of every day! Through Jesus I am reconciled to God and brought into a relationship with the One who answers each of the questions I find posed in Job 38. The Lord's answer is a resounding I AM!

> *Who enclosed the sea behind doors*
> *when it burst from the womb,*
> *when I made the clouds its garment*
> *and thick darkness its blanket,*

*when I determined its boundaries
and put its bars and doors in place,
when I declared: You may come this far, but no farther;
your proud waves stop here.* —Job 38:8-11 (HCSB)

We need a daily reality check. We need to know and acknowledge that there is One who is greater than we are—mightier, more powerful, and *more* in all things and in all ways. Yet, the Mighty One in His great love and mercy sent His Son to restore us into a right relationship with Him, a relationship that is personal and intimate. His name is the LORD God, Jehovah, and He alone is worthy of all praise!

SHINE
What or who are you boasting in today? Are your attempts to control life leaving you frustrated and frazzled? Are you operating in your own strength and finding yourself worn out and weary? Pour out your heart to the God who is awesome in might and power, and yet near to all who call on Him in truth. Reflect on the verses from today and on the fact that God is the Lord of Hosts, Almighty and All-Powerful! Boast in who He is to someone today.

10

Day 10 — He is For Us!

SOAK
Deep calls to deep at the roar of your waterfalls; all your breakers and your waves have gone over me. —Psalm 42:7

Read Psalm 42.

Have you ever found yourself asking some of the same questions this Psalmist poses?

- Why am I so depressed?
- Why all this turmoil within me?
- Where are You, God?
- Why have You forgotten me?
- Why must I go about in sorrow?

I know I have. I have been in that place where it felt as if the waves and waterfalls were rushing over me. But in the depths of darkness God's presence was there—the deepest parts of my heart and soul exposed to the One who created me. Out of the depths I cried out to the Creator and He was there. He IS there.

I love this psalm because it is real and transparent. I love how the author is in conversation with himself—you know that "self-talk". We all do it. But it is the perspective that we find in the psalm that is so helpful and healing to us. It begins with the opening verse and the psalmist's declaration and acknowledgement of his need for God. He longs for, thirsts for, and craves God's presence. Then all of the questioning, confession of his depression, and inner turmoil follows. But did you notice the repeated phrase found after the questioning?

Put your hope in God, for I will still praise Him, my Savior and my God!

God knows us intimately. He knows our thoughts, our feelings, our desires, and our dreams. He created us (Psalm 139). He implores us to pour out our hearts to Him because He is our refuge (Psalm 62:8). But we must also KNOW who He is—His character, His nature, and His ways. When we are grounded in the truth of who God is, we can come through the waves and breakers that wash over us and stand again. As someone who suffers from bouts of depression, I know how good this kind of "self-talk" can be in my life. It is how I process. It is simply a conversation with God. I also know how crucial it is for me to KNOW my God! I love that we find so many names and attributes of God in this psalm. He is the living God, my rock, my Savior, the LORD who is faithful love and the God of my life.

Growing in my knowledge of God is not only to occur when things get tough but on a daily basis as I renew my mind with the truths of His Word. Then, when the waves hit and I feel as if I am drowning underneath them I am ready and more prepared. I can pour out my heart and acknowledge my difficult situation, but with the resolve that I will still praise Him because He is my God, my rock, my Savior! That resolve comes not only as I renew my mind in the truths of God's Word, but as a result of my relationship with Jesus and all He has done for me. He has conquered sin and overcome it all—even death. He has given me hope and an eternal future in God's presence. All that happens on this side of eternity is simply to make me more like Jesus and to reflect God's glory—but with the assurance that He is with me and He is for me. It is this assurance that enables me to rise above the waters and roaring waves and say, I will still praise Him, my Savior and my God!

Little children, you are from God and have overcome them, for He who is in you is greater than He who is in the world. —1 John 4:4

What then shall we say to these things? If God is for us, who can be against us? ...Who shall separate us from the love of Christ? Shall tribulation, or distress, or persecution, or famine, or nakedness, or danger, or sword? ...No, in all these things we are more than conquerors through him who loved us. For I am sure that neither death nor life, nor angels nor rulers, nor things present nor things to come, nor powers, nor height nor depth, nor anything else in all creation, will be able to separate us from the love of God in Christ Jesus our Lord. —Romans 8:31, 35,37-39

SHINE

Do you need to know God as the living God, your Savior, your rock, the One who is faithful love and abundant hope? Consider your current situation in light of who God is and praise Him. Your circumstances may not change, but your perspective and attitude will—and that changes everything. Reflect on the verses from today and on the fact that God is for you. He is always present and your refuge.

Day 11 — He Calms the Storms!

SOAK

But He said to them, "Why are you fearful, you of little faith?" Then He got up and rebuked the winds and the sea. And there was a great calm.
—Matthew 8:26 (HCSB)

Read Matthew 8:23-27.

Notice how Jesus addressed His disciples in this passage. He points out how small and weak their faith is, *you of little faith*. Fear is the opposite of faith. Faith is trusting and believing God. It is taking Him at His Word and walking in the power of His presence moment by moment. But how often I find myself fretting and fearful instead of turning to and trusting God with my concerns and fears. Yet, I want to be a woman who trusts and believes God, and takes Him at His Word in all things.

I have seen and experienced His faithfulness and trustworthiness in my life confirmed time and again through the years. But I still find myself fearful and fretting at times. When I feel that fear rising in me, it is a cue for me to turn to God. It is a reminder to confess that my fear is a lack of trust and faith. It prompts me to cry out to the Lord in prayer and praise Him! When I do this, it always calms my fears and floods my soul with the peace that only He can provide. It becomes a practice in my life because I know fear will tempt me once again to look to my circumstances instead of to my God. But when fear rises up in me again, I just repeat the process. This is one reason the study of God's names and attributes, making it a daily practice to acknowledge who HE IS, is so important in our lives. Fear, and the obstacles looming large in our sight, shrinks when we make much of God—which is exactly what praising and glorifying God is all about.

Now the eye of the LORD is on those who fear Him—those who depend on His faithful love to deliver them from death and to keep from alive in famine. —Psalm 33:18-19 (HCSB)

Read Psalm 33 dividing it up into the sections noted below. At the end of each section, pause and respond with prayers of praise and adoration to God for who He is.

Read Psalm 33:1-5. Pause and praise!
Read Psalm 33:6-11. Pause and praise!
Read Psalm 33:12-22. Pause and praise!

The counsel of the Lord stands forever, the plans of His heart from generation to generation. —Psalm 33:11 (HCSB)

He alone shapes their hearts; He considers all their works. —Psalm 33:15 (HCSB)

Now the eye of the Lord is on those who fear Him—those who depend on His faithful love. To deliver them from death and to keep from alive in famine. —Psalm 33:18-19 (HCSB)

We wait for Yahweh; He is our help and shield. For our hearts rejoice in Him because we trust in His holy name. May Your faithful love rest on us, Yahweh, for we put our hope in You. —Psalm 33:20-22 (HCSB)

SHINE
What fears and fretfulness are you experiencing today? Stop and confess your fear as a lack of trust and belief in God, and then spend some time praising Him! He will rebuke the winds and waves of fear that are washing over you and flood you with His peace and joy. Reflect on the verses from today and on the fact that God is greater than your fears and with you in all the storms of life.

12

Day 12 — Who is Strong like You, Lord?

SOAK

For who in the skies can be compared to the LORD? Who among the heavenly beings is like the LORD, a God greatly to be feared in the council of the holy ones, and awesome above all who are around him? O LORD God of hosts, who is mighty as you are, O LORD, with your faithfulness all around you? You rule the raging of the sea; when its waves rise, you still them. —Psalm 89:6-9

Read Psalm 89:1-19.

Today I want us to simply soak in the Word. Read slowly. Let God's words and presence wash over you. Pause and meditate upon the words of God. Respond in praise and adoration of our Mighty God! Take His living and active Word with you as you go about your day and remember: *From the rising of the sun to its setting, the name of the Lord is to be praised!* —Psalm 113:3.

Make a list of the characteristics and names of God found in Psalm 89.
Use this list in your prayer time to praise and adore God for who He is and what He has done.

SHINE
Reflect on the verses from today and praise your Mighty God! Pray back to the Lord the attributes of His character you found in Psalm 89. Praise Him. Encourage someone today with the truth that God is mighty!

Day 13 — His Mighty Strength

SOAK

You faithfully answer our prayers with awesome deeds, O God our Savior. You are the hope of everyone on earth, even those who sail on distant seas. You formed the mountains by your power and armed yourself with mighty strength. You quieted the raging oceans with their pounding waves and silenced the shouting of the nations. Those who live at the ends of the earth stand in awe of your wonders. From where the sun rises to where it sets, you inspire shouts of joy. —Psalm 65:5-8 (NLT)

Read Psalm 65:1-8. According to this passage, what do you learn about how God acts? What do you learn about His character and nature?

We see that God...
- Hears our prayers
- Forgives our sins
- Satisfies us
- Faithfully answers us
- Is our hope
- Formed the mountains with power and mighty strength
- Quiets the raging oceans and their pounding waves
- Silences the shouts of the nations

What struck me most in this passage is back in verse 3, *Though we are overwhelmed by our sins, you forgive them all.* In the original language, the word *overwhelm or prevail* (depending on your translation) means *to have strength, be strong, be powerful, be mighty, be great, to prevail.*

The more aware I am of God's presence and His holiness and goodness, the more I see myself for who I am apart from Him—small, powerless, and sinful. In His presence I come face to face with the overwhelming reality of my sin on a daily basis and how powerless I am to defeat it in my own strength. Yet this great and glorious God chose to send His Son Jesus to die, atone for, and forgive all the sin in my life. What I was unable to do for myself, He has done for me in His great mercy, love, and power (Ephesians 2:1-9). He has done this for you as well!

I surrendered control of my life to Jesus in my early 30's and I had made quite a mess of things before this time. Sin had certainly overwhelmed my life and almost destroyed everything of value in it. I can relate to sin being powerful, strong, and beyond my ability to conquer. But God being rich in His mercy redeemed, restored, and renewed my life.

Even as a Christian, I battle sin on a daily basis. My feet hardly hit the floor each morning before I have had an unkind thought, spoken a word that tears down instead of builds up, grumbled, complained, been selfish, or self-serving. As Christ-followers we still walk about in this body of flesh and live in a fallen world—we will battle sin. But in Jesus, sin no longer has dominion over us (Romans 6:6-14)! This means sin no longer has the power to rule, defeat, or destroy because Jesus has provided a means of escape. When we acknowledge and confess our sins, He is faithful and just to forgive! (1 John 4:9)

The daily realization of this fact causes the words of Psalm 65:8 to resonate with my heart and soul, to the very depths of my being!

[We] stand in awe...from where the sun rises to where it sets, You inspire shouts of joy! —Psalm 65:8 (NLT)

I stand in awe! He inspires shouts of joy in my life. In His great might and power God not only creates, upholds, and sustain all things, but has provided for my greatest need in life—forgiveness, restoration, renewal, and hope.

SHINE
Reflect on the verses from today. Praise Him today as Mighty God, the One who in His mighty strength and unfailing love has provided forgiveness for your sins and has restored you into a right relationship with Him.

Day 14 — The Lord Reigns!

SOAK

The LORD reigns! He is robed in majesty; The LORD is robed, enveloped in strength. The world is firmly established; it cannot be shaken. Your throne has been established from the beginning; You are from eternity. The floods have lifted up, LORD, the floods have lifted up their voice; the floods lift up their pounding waves. Greater than the roar of many waters —the mighty breakers of the sea—the LORD on high is majestic. LORD, Your testimonies are completely reliable; holiness is the beauty of Your house for all the days to come. —Psalm 93:1-5 (HCSB)

Read Psalm 93.

A shaky world is a reality to which we can all relate in one way or another. Perhaps your world is shaking in your job, your marriage, your parenting, your relationships, your finances, or your health. Psalm 93 assures us that the Lord reigns. He is in control. He is Creator and Sustainer. Even in the midst of the mountains shaking, the waves pounding, and the water roaring the Lord is on high. He is powerful and mighty. Even when we cannot see with natural eyes, we can rest in His power and might knowing He is sure, steadfast, and sovereign over all things.

Therefore let us be grateful for receiving a kingdom that cannot be shaken, and thus let us offer to God acceptable worship, with reverence and awe. —Hebrews 12:28

Even in the midst of a shaky world we find security, hope, and comfort in Jesus' presence. When our world is shaking, there are some practical ways we can choose to respond. We find them in Hebrews 12:1-3.

Therefore, since we are surrounded by so great a cloud of witnesses, let us also lay aside every weight, and sin which clings so closely, and let us run with endurance the race that is set before us, looking to Jesus, the founder and perfecter of our faith, who for the joy that was set before him endured the cross, despising the shame, and is seated at the right hand of the throne of God. —Hebrews 12:1-3

Let us...
- lay aside the sin (*we looked at this yesterday*)
- run with endurance the race (the life) before us
- look to Jesus

We run with perseverance—not in our own strength or stamina, but by seeking Jesus and relying on the power and strength of the Holy Spirit at work within us.

We look to Jesus! I love the definition in the original language for the word *look* in this verse. It means *to turn the eyes away from other things and fix them on something.*

When my world is shaking, the waves are pounding, and waters are roaring, I look to Jesus. I turn my attention from the shaking and fix my mind on the One who is strong and secure, robed in strength and power. Jesus created, sustains, and upholds all things! When I shift my gaze and fix my thoughts on Jesus, my heart and soul find calm, peace, and strength in the midst of the storm.

For by Him all things were created, in heaven and on earth, visible and invisible, whether thrones or dominions or rulers or authorities — all things were created through Him and for Him. And He is before all things, and in Him all things hold together. —Colossians 1:16-17

SHINE
Reflect on the verses from today and on the fact that God is unshakeable! When you look to Him and lay your fears at His feet, you can find calm and peace in the midst of the storms of life and a shaky world.

Sweet Summer Treats

Summer foods! Cool lemonade over ice on those sizzling hot days and kids setting up their lemonade stands on the neighborhood street corner. Evenings on the back porch making homemade ice cream. After dinner trips to the frozen yogurt shop or juicy watermelons dripping with sticky goodness on a summer afternoon.

This week, let's allow the imagery of those delightfully good summer treats to prompt us to praise God for His goodness.

15

Day 15 — He is Good

SOAK

Good. It is an overused word in our language. When someone asks how we are doing and we respond "good", it can convey a wide range of thoughts and feelings.

- I'm doing okay.
- I'm having a lousy day, but don't feel like talking about it.
- I'm being polite.
- Nothing special, nothing traumatic, I'm just here.

When we are rating or grading something, good is usually considered mediocre—not poor and not excellent. But when we speak of the goodness of God, it is nothing like our trivial overuse of the word.

God's goodness is infinite, perfect, and unchanging. Psalm 119:68 sums it up beautifully and simply, *You are good and all You do is good.*

Read Psalm 34:1-22.

In Psalm 34:8 we are encouraged to *"taste and see that the Lord is good"*. Think of some of the things you enjoy tasting in summertime—ice cream, cold lemonade, watermelon, and fresh summer fruits. This week, let's *taste and see* the goodness of God.

In Psalm 34:8 the word for *taste,* in the original language of the Old Testament, means *to perceive and experience.* The word for *see* means *to look at or view, but with the idea of to learn, experience, examine, investigate, discover and to enjoy.*

God invites us to experience and enjoy His goodness. It is a delight like no other! Psalm 119:103-104 says,
"How sweet are your words to my taste, sweeter than honey to my mouth! I gain understanding from your precepts."

33

God's Word is a delight and through it God reveals to us who He is. Through His Word we are given the opportunity to know, experience, and enjoy Him. We were created to praise and glorify God. We will spend eternity delighting in God and enjoying His presence. (Isaiah 43:7)

Read Psalm 34 and make a list of the ways God shows His goodness to His children. Look for the "when I..." statements and then note the Lord's response to those situations. In this Psalm we are given some specific ways to *taste and see* the Lord's goodness.

Read Psalm 34:8-10. List the three instructions you find that help us *taste and see that the Lord is good?* (Hint: look for verbs/actions). List the corresponding benefits that follow when we do these things.

SHINE

Throughout your day, look for opportunities to *taste and see* that the Lord is good! Experience, discover, and enjoy His goodness and respond with praise and thanksgiving. Reflect on the verses from today and on the fact that God is good!

16

Day 16 — What Has God's Goodness Done for You?

SOAK

Oftentimes we can become mentally fixated on our circumstances and the problems flooding our lives in the moment. We lose sight of all that God has done for us. We lose sight of His goodness.

Today, renew your heart and soul in truth and *taste and see* all that God has done for you in Christ Jesus. This renewal will give you a fresh, new perspective on your circumstances.

But when the goodness and loving kindness of God our Savior appeared, he saved us, not because of works done by us in righteousness, but according to his own mercy, by the washing of regeneration and renewal of the Holy Spirit, whom he poured out on us richly through Jesus Christ our Savior, so that being justified by his grace we might become heirs according to the hope of eternal life. —Titus 3:4-7

Moses said, 'Please show me your glory." And he said, "I will make all my goodness pass before you and will proclaim before you my name 'The LORD ' And I will be gracious to whom I will be gracious, and will show mercy on whom I will show mercy...The LORD descended in the cloud and stood with him there, and proclaimed the name of the LORD. The LORD passed before him and proclaimed, 'The LORD, the LORD, a God merciful and gracious, slow to anger, and abounding in steadfast love and faithfulness.' —Exodus 33:18-19, 34:5-6

Read the following verses and make a list of what they teach you about all the good God has accomplished in your life:
- Titus 3:4-7
- Ephesians 2:1-10
- Ephesians 1:3-14 — holy - blameless - predestined - redemption
- Colossians 1:21-23
- 2 Corinthians 5:17-21
- Romans 8:28-31

Complete the following statement based on what you've just read: *God's goodness in my life has accomplished* _____.

Read 1 Peter 2:2-3. What are we to do as those who have tasted the Lord's goodness?

What is your response to the goodness of God in your life?

Trust
Thankfulness

SHINE
Reflect on the verses from today and on the fact that God is good! Remember that He is working even in the midst of difficult circumstances. Praise Him for His goodness in your life. Make a list of things for which you are thankful and watch how it changes your perspective. Share with someone today at least one good thing the Lord has done in your life.

Day 17 — He is Greater!

SOAK

Praise the LORD, for the LORD is good; sing to his name, for it is pleasant!
—Psalm 135:3

Are there times in life when you have trouble seeing the goodness of God? I think we've all had moments, circumstances and even seasons when we've wondered what God was doing and where He was in the midst of it all. Undoubtedly, there will be things in this life we will never fully understand and that cause us to wonder how God can bring good out of the situation.

But His thoughts are not our thoughts, and His ways are not our ways (Isaiah 55:8-9). We can rest and trust in the promises of His Word and who He is, even when we don't fully understand the why and see the good with our earthly eyes.

We are confident that God is able to orchestrate everything to work toward something good and beautiful when we love Him and accept His invitation to live according to His plan. From the distant past, His eternal love reached into the future. You see, He knew those who would be His one day, and He chose them beforehand to be conformed to the image of His Son so that Jesus would be the firstborn of a new family of believers, all brothers and sisters. As for those He chose beforehand, He called them to a different destiny so that they would experience what it means to be made right with God and share in His glory. So what should we say about all of this? If God is on our side, then tell me: whom should we fear? — Romans 8:28-31 (The Voice)

There are times in my life when distractions keep me from seeing God's goodness. I make the things of this world more important and greater in my sight. I get too focused on and try to find satisfaction in worldly things—those things that are temporal and will not endure for eternity. I lose sight of who God is. Praise refocuses my gaze and gives me a new perspective.

Read Psalm 135:1-9. What do you learn about the goodness and greatness of God in this passage?

Read Psalm 135:15-18.
These verses give us a word picture and description of idols or other gods. How do the idols, other gods, compare to what we learn about who God is in verses 1-8? Remember, idols in our lives are not just carved images, but anything to which we assign greater worth or significance than we do God. It is anything we turn to instead of God.

Read Psalm 145:14-16, Psalm 17:15 and Psalm 90:14. According to these verses, what truly satisfies us and who or what should we be focused upon? How do these verses help us to trust God and His goodness even when life is hard and the good is difficult to discern?

SHINE
Sing His praises! Reflect on the verses from today and on the fact that God is good and He alone can satisfy the deepest longings of your heart and life.

For I know that the LORD is great, and that our Lord is above all gods. — Psalm 135:5

Day 18 — He is Good...Say SO!

SOAK
Give thanks to the LORD, for He is good; His faithful love endures forever.
—Psalm 107:1 (HCSB)

In Christ Jesus we are redeemed from our empty way of life, our sins are forgiven and we are restored into a right relationship with God. As those redeemed, we are to proclaim His goodness. We are to share with others the goodness of God and what His goodness has done for us and in us. Psalm 107 gives us a great example to follow. Today we will work through the Psalm in sections.

Read through Psalm 107 in the following sections: Psalm 107:4-9, 107:10-16, 107:17-22, 107:23-32.
For each section of Scripture, complete the statements:

They _____.
God did _____.
For God is _____.

Let the redeemed of the Lord *Say SO!* Did you see that God satisfies us, shatters our chains of bondage, sends His Word and heals, stills the storms, and brings us to safe refuge in His presence? And that is just a drop in the bucket!

What is your redemption story? Use the examples from Psalm 107 and the statements above to write your own *Say SO!* story.

One of the best ways we can *Say SO!* is by cultivating an attitude of gratitude. Psalm 107 instructs us to not only tell our story, but to also give thanks. We are told throughout the New Testament that giving thanks should be a habit of one who follows Jesus. (Ephesians 5:4, Philippians 4:6, Colossians 2:7, Colossians 4:2, 1 Thessalonians 3:9, 1 Timothy 2:1, 1 Timothy 4:3-4, 2 Corinthians 4:15).

In the original language of the New Testament, the word for *give thanks* or *be thankful* means to *give thanks, to be grateful, mindful of favors, it is grateful language; active language to God as an act of worship.* This word is in the present tense, imperative mood and active voice. Hang with me! This means it is a command and a continuous, repeated action. The active voice means YOU do it!

Is your day characterized more by grateful language or grumbling language?

Give thanks in all circumstances; for this is the will of God in Christ Jesus for you. —1 Thessalonians 5:18

Remembering to *Say SO!* and cultivating an attitude of gratitude always takes my eyes off whatever is causing me to grumble, complain, be discontent, discouraged, disappointed or dissatisfied and to look to and praise my God—who is GOOD!

SHINE
Reflect on the verses from today and on the fact that God is good and His goodness endures forever. *Say SO* today! Tell someone your redemption story.

19

Day 19 — While you Wait...

SOAK

I believe that I shall look upon the goodness of the LORD in the land of the living! Wait for the LORD; be strong, and let your heart take courage; wait for the LORD. —Psalm 27:13-14

Do you have dreams, desires or expectations that have yet to be fulfilled? Are there disappointed longings in your life? Is there a specific request you have been waiting patiently on God to answer? Are you in the midst of a difficult circumstance that you wish would just be over? Is there something for which you are groaning and yearning? Do you feel like a plane in a holding pattern...circling...waiting to land?

Waiting can be difficult. Our culture promotes the idea of instant gratification everywhere we turn. But waiting can be a good thing and not just a time of idle fretfulness, impatience or discouragement.

Read Psalm 27.

I want us to focus on a few key words from this Psalm and their definitions in the original language of the Old Testament:

Goodness means *goodness, fairness, and beauty.* The root concept of this noun is that of desirability for enjoyment.

Wait means *to look eagerly for, to lie in wait for, to wait for, linger for, to collect and to bind together.*

Take refuge means *to strengthen, prevail, be strong, become strong, be courageous, be firm, grow firm, and to be resolute.*

The psalmist exclaims that even in his difficulty and uncertainty he believes he will see the goodness of God in the land of the living. Here on earth, even amidst all the sin and brokenness, we can find goodness. As I hope you've discovered this week, our source of all that is good is God

41

Himself.

What good can come while we wait and how can we make our "wait time" productive?

God's Word calls us to wait upon Him—to bind ourselves to Him, to cling to Him and to seek refuge while we wait in His presence. Waiting can be a very good thing and God is always working in our waiting.

Read through the verses listed below on *waiting*. How do these verses encourage you as you wait? What are some practical things you can do *while you wait?*
- Psalm 62:5
- Psalm 130:5
- Isaiah 26:8
- Lamentations 3:24-25
- Isaiah 40:31
- Psalm 31:19-21

How great is Your goodness that You have stored up for those who fear You and accomplished in the sight of everyone for those who take refuge in You. You hide them in the protection of Your presence; You conceal them in a shelter from the schemes of men, from quarrelsome tongues. May the LORD be praised, for He has wonderfully shown His faithful love to me in a city under siege. —Psalm 31:19-21 (HCSB)

The LORD is good, a stronghold in the day of trouble; he knows those who take refuge in him. —Nahum 1:7

SHINE
Reflect on the verses from today and pondering the fact, God IS good. It is not just that He does good, but His very nature and essence IS good. Praise Him for His goodness today.

20

Day 20 — He is Great...Tell Someone!

SOAK
The LORD is good to all, and his mercy is over all that he has made.
—Psalm 145:9

Psalm 145 is a wonderful song of praise declaring who God is and what He has done for us. His goodness in our lives should prompt us to not only praise Him, but to also declare His goodness to others. What steps are you taking to declare His goodness to the next generation?

Read Psalm 145.

What does the greatness of God cause us to do? (verses 3-12)

How do we see the greatness and goodness of the Lord in action in verses 13-20?

How have you seen the mercy of God at work in your own life?

SHINE
Reflect on the verses from today and on the fact that God is good and merciful! Look for opportunities today to declare the goodness of God and to share who He is and what He has done with anyone He places in your path.

21

Day 21 — His Goodness Endures!

SOAK

For the Lord is good; his steadfast love endures forever, and his faithfulness to all generations. —Psalm 100:5

Today I want us to focus on another aspect of God's goodness and one that is central to His character—His steadfast love, or my favorite translation from the New International Version (NIV), His **unfailing** love. Some translations may also use the word, *mercy.*

In a fallen world marked by sin, it is so encouraging to me that my God is unfailing in His love and faithfulness toward me. It gives me hope to know that even in my faithlessness and failings, God is still unfailing love toward me. And Jesus is the source of that hope!

In the original language of the Old Testament, the word, *unfailing love,* means *kindness, loving kindness, mercy, goodness, faithfulness, love, acts of kindness.*

The *Complete Word Study Bible Dictionary* gives us further insight on this word, "*This aspect of God is one of several important features of His character: truth; faithfulness; mercy; steadfastness; justice; righteousness; goodness. Unfailing love implies personal involvement and it is covenantal with those God has chosen and redeemed. It implies reciprocity, but since God's love is ultimately beyond the covenant, it will not be abandoned even when the human partner is unfaithful.*"

We find God's unfailing love often tied to His faithfulness in Scripture.

Psalm 136 is a wonderful passage for understanding God's steadfast and unfailing love. Unfailing love is used 26 times in this passage.

Read Psalm 136 in the sections shown below. Note what you learn about this aspect of God's character. What connections do you see between God's unfailing love and His faithfulness? How does this encourage you today?

- Psalm 136:1-3
- Psalm 136:4-9
- Psalm 136:10-15
- Psalm 136:16
- Psalm 136:17-22
- Psalm 136:23-25
- Psalm 136:26

*Praise the **LORD**! Oh give thanks to the **LORD**, for he is good, for his steadfast love endures forever.* —Psalm 106:1

SHINE
Reflect on the verses from today and on the unfailing love and faithfulness of God. Share with someone today how you have seen God's unfailing love demonstrated in your life.

The Joys of Summer

One of my favorite things about summertime is going barefoot—and the next best thing is wearing flip flops. I love them! Flip flops would be my year-round footwear of choice if it were practical (*it almost is here in Georgia*). I find joy in the simple things of summer—flip flops, going barefoot in the summer grass or on a sandy beach, the sound and smell of summer rain. This week let's focus on those things we associate with summertime which bring a smile to our face. Let's use these images to prompt us to praise God, who IS joy! He is our reason for rejoicing. He is our ultimate source of satisfaction and delight. Let's rejoice in His presence this week.

22

Day 22 — True Joy!

SOAK

You make known to me the path of life; in your presence there is fullness of joy; at your right hand are pleasures forevermore. —Psalm 16:11

Joy! We all want it in our lives but at times it can seem to allude us. Too often we base our joy on our circumstances and feelings.

True joy is not the same as the world's definition for happiness. Happiness is from the root word, *hap*, meaning *by chance or circumstances*. Our joy is not based on happenstance or circumstance; our joy is based on a restored relationship with God through Jesus. And He IS sovereign, all-knowing, all-powerful and ever-present!

Psalm 43:4 uses one of my favorite descriptive names of God.
Then I will go to the altar of my God, to God my exceeding joy and I will praise you with the lyre, O God, my God.

God my exceeding joy translates as *El Simha Giyl*. It means *God, rejoicing joy*. Giyl in the original language conveys the word picture of twirling. I love this idea! It is a wild joy—amazing, incredible, and unrestrained.

This place of wild joy—in God's presence—is a place that is not bound by circumstance, time or feelings. It is the place of "in spite of". It is the place where we can turn when we are troubled or discouraged, facing difficult people or circumstances, whether we have much or little, when things go our way and when they don't, when we are feeling sad, happy, or something in between. It is a place that is constant and enduring because this place is the presence of the ONE who is constant and enduring—our Lord God, *El Simhah Giyl*!

Psalm 43:5 goes on to ask, *Why are you cast down, O my soul, and why are you in turmoil within me? Hope in God; for I shall again praise him, my salvation and my God.*

Joy is the overflow of my relationship with God, therefore I need to cultivate that relationship. Joy is found as I seek God's presence through prayer and His Word. Joy is found as I seek to live in obedience to God's Word and to imitate Christ. Joy is found as I yield to the Holy Spirit and His control in my life.

SHINE

Reflect on the verses from today and on the fact that God is your wild joy! This joy is not bound by circumstance, time or feelings. This joy is yours in Christ Jesus! If your present situation seems out of control and your mood is cast down, remember God is *El Simhah Giyl*, your rejoicing joy. Get up and dance, twirl and rejoice in God's presence!

23

Day 23 — A Joyful Retreat for the Soul!

SOAK

A retreat! I love those words. We all need a retreat from time to time to refresh and renew us. For some it may be a bubble bath at the end of a long day, a good book, a cup of tea, a workout at the gym or a long weekend getaway. For many of us, our favorite places of retreat in the summertime are the beaches or mountains. But every day can be a joyful retreat that refreshes, renews, restores and leaves a lasting impression on those around us.

> *I rejoice at your word like one who discovers a great treasure.*
> *—Psalm 119:162 (NLT)*

Read Hebrews 4:12 and Psalm 19:7-11.

These verses paint a great word picture of how God's Word is a spa for our soul and spirit. God's word is like fresh water flowing over our hearts and souls as it refines and smoothes out the rough edges. God's Word is a healing balm to our wounded and weary hearts. It is a daily retreat where we can enjoy the refreshing presence of God that leaves us changed and renewed. Take a look at some of the ways God's Word is a spa day for our souls.

Rejuvenates:

Hebrews 4:12 tells us that the word of God is *living and active*. These words actually mean *to have life, to be alive, energy, capable of doing, power, engaged in work*. God's Word is energy to our soul and spirit. It is actively working in us to bring about life. It rejuvenates us when we are tired, weary, distraught, overwhelmed, fearful, worried, or burdened.

Reveals:

We also read in Hebrews 4:12 that God's Word judges the thoughts and intentions of our hearts. It is like an exfoliation for our hearts and souls. It exposes areas of wrong thinking, wrong attitudes, and areas where the enemy has taken us captive in our thoughts. It reveals areas of our lives that are not wholeheartedly devoted to Jesus.

Revives:
Did you notice the ways God's Word is described in Psalm 19:7-11? It says it *revives the soul, enlightens the eyes, rejoices the heart, making wise, and tastes sweeter than honey.* These are great mental word pictures of the rejuvenating and reviving power of God's Word in our lives.

When we read, study, and meditate upon the Word of God we are able to recognize the lies that are keeping us captive. The lies that are hindering our growth are exposed. God's Word reveals areas of our lives we need to surrender and truth we need to apply and live out. God uses His Word to expose and then restore us so that we reflect Jesus more.

Renews:
Read Romans 12:1-2. We are transformed (changed) as we renew our mind in God's Word. This enables us to discern God's will. He changes our attitudes, thoughts, words and actions—all through the power of His Spirit at work within us and His powerful and energizing word of Truth.

SHINE
Could you use some rejuvenation in your life? Do you need to be refreshed in your soul and spirit? Spend some time today renewing your mind and reviving your heart and soul in God's Word. Reflect on the verses from today and on the fact that God's Word brings joy to your life!

During your praise time let the closing verses of **Psalm 19** be your prayer:

Who can discern his errors? Declare me innocent from hidden faults. Keep back your servant also from presumptuous sins; let them not have dominion over me! Then I shall be blameless, and innocent of great transgression. Let the words of my mouth and the meditation of my heart be acceptable in your sight, O LORD, my rock and my redeemer.

Day 24 — A Refuge for Rejoicing in the Storm

SOAK

I love lighthouses on the beach. I love their shapes and colors and what they represent. They provide a guiding light to the safe haven of the shore. They are constructed to withstand the storms and waves that beat upon them. Ships at sea can depend upon the beacon of the lighthouse to direct them home. They are a refuge.

This prompts me to evaluate my own life and ask: What or who am I relying upon? Who or in what am I trusting? Is my reliance upon God alone or in other things? Is He my refuge? Does He direct, control and suggest the activities of my day?

But let all who take refuge in You rejoice; let them shout for joy forever. May You shelter them, and may those who love Your name boast about You. —Psalm 5:11 (HCSB)

God's presence is a place of refuge and protection, of peace, comfort, hope, and strength. It is a place of joy.

Those who know your name trust in you, for you, LORD, have never forsaken those who seek you —Psalm 9:10 (NIV)

In Him our hearts rejoice for we trust in His holy name.
—Psalm 33:21 (HCSB)

Trust in the LORD with all your heart and do not lean on your own understanding. In all your ways acknowledge Him, and He will make your paths straight. —Proverbs 3:5-6 (NASB)

Did you notice the repeated word in each of those verses? Trust. In the original language of the Old Testament, the word, *trust,* means *to go quickly [to hie] for refuge; to trust in, to have confidence, to be bold, to be secure, to feel safe.*

We find joy when we trust God—who He is and what He has done. Trust is simply taking God at His Word, acknowledging who He is, and stepping out in faith. We cannot always see the shore. We don't always know the details of the plan. 1 Peter 1:6-9 acknowledges the fact that we will have trouble in this life. We will face various trials and our lives will be shaken at times. But it goes on to tell us that "even though" we cannot see and know all of the details, or even the outcome of our situation, we can experience inexpressible joy.

Our trials and hardship can cause us to look at life from the perspective of "what if..." or "if only..." and neither of these will bring us joy and peace. Neither of these are a refuge for our weary hearts and souls. 1 Peter 1:8 tells us we experience inexpressible joy as we love and believe (trust) God regardless of the circumstance or feelings in the moment. Loving and believing God in the midst of the "even though" will cause us to leap and dance with gladness, to experience a joy that is a delight and pleasure that is inexpressible. Our rejoicing is full of glory, meaning it brings glory to God.

Too often our tendency is to seek refuge in things other than the presence of God and His Word. But God calls us to "take refuge" in Him. I know...I can hear the "but" questions rumbling in your head:

What about when I am stressed? **Take Refuge!**

What about when I can't pay my bills? **Take Refuge!**

What about when I am facing a battle with no strength left? **Take Refuge!**

What about when I see wrong/evil prevailing? **Take Refuge!**

What about when my marriage is in trouble? **Take Refuge!**

What about when my children won't obey or make poor choices? **Take Refuge!**

What about when my health is failing? **Take Refuge!**

What about when I'm in that trial or difficulty to which I see no end? **Take Refuge!**

What about when I have a decision to make and need wisdom and answers? **Take Refuge!**

Lord, You have been our refuge in every generation. —*Psalm 90:1 (HCSB)*

SHINE
Reflect on the verses from today and on the fact that God is a refuge you can trust and His presence brings joy. If any of the above "what about when…" statements resonate with you, take them to the Lord. Praise and thank Him for being your refuge. Rejoice and give thanks that you can always run to and rejoice in God's presence.

25

Day 25 — Celebrate the Day!

SOAK
This is the day that the LORD has made; let us rejoice and be glad in it.
— Psalm 118:24

You want to be joyful and celebrate...but you're just not feeling it today. Life is overwhelming. Life is blah. Life is hard. You're tired. You're empty. How do you find joy and celebrate the day?

Scripture instructs us to *be joyful always* (1 Thessalonians 5:16) even in the midst of difficulties. James 1:2 exhorts us to *count it all joy when we face trials of many kinds.*

How do we experience the joy that surpasses our circumstances and feelings?
God allows trials and hardships in our lives so that we might come to Him, rely upon Him, and experience His presence (2 Corinthians 1:8). We were created for fellowship with God Almighty, the Creator, Sustainer, Redeemer and All Powerful One. His presence is splendid, glorious, and intoxicating!

Experiencing the joy and strength found in the presence of the Lord each day is a *choice* we make. It is all about the perspective we choose to take. We can choose to celebrate the day that the Lord has made—resting and trusting in His presence—or we can choose to fret, fear, and be frustrated.

I love the encouragement and exhortation we find in Hebrews 12:1-2: *Therefore, since we are surrounded by so great a cloud of witnesses, let us also lay aside every weight, and sin which clings so closely, and let us run with endurance the race that is set before us, looking to Jesus, the founder and perfecter of our faith, who for the joy that was set before him endured the cross, despising the shame, and is seated at the right hand of the throne of God.*

Looking to Jesus! The word in the original language for *looking to* is one of my favorite word pictures. The word means *to turn the eyes away from other things and fix them on something.* When life is hard and joy seems impossible, we change our perspective and attitude by *looking to Jesus.* When I look to Him, I have to take my eyes off other things! I fix my eyes on Him. He becomes my focus and changes my perspective, regardless of the situation.

It is up to you...how will you choose to spend this day? Where will you choose to focus your gaze?

Satisfy us in the morning with your steadfast love, that we may rejoice and be glad all our days. —Psalm 90:14

SHINE
Reflect on the verses from today and on the fact that God is your joy regardless of how you are feeling or what you are facing! Get out in God's creation and look up and around you. Rejoice and praise Him, not only for who He is, but for all that He has made for you to enjoy!

26

Day 26 — Seeking Joy!

SOAK

Glory in his holy name; let the hearts of those who seek the LORD rejoice; seek the LORD and his strength; seek his presence continually.
—Psalm 105:3-4

Read Psalm 105:3-4 and answer the following questions based on the text.

What are we instructed to do?
What are we to seek?
How often?
What is the result?

Seek is repeated three times in this passage and two different words are used in the original language.

The first and third occurrence is the word, *baqash,* meaning *to seek, to desire, to require, to request, to seek to find or secure; to go to God especially with prayer.*

The second occurrence is the word, *darash,* meaning *to beat a path, to tread, to frequent a place; to resort to, to seek, to look, to investigate, to practice, study and follow, to seek with application.*

God's presence is always with us, but do we always practice the presence of the Lord? When we seek His presence, we find joy and strength. We are not to tread this path of life in our own strength. We are to walk in the strength and power of the Lord's presence.

What promises does God give to those who seek His presence? Look at a few cross-reference verses:

- He will never forsake those who trust and seek Him. (Psalm 9:10)
- Those who seek His presence will lack no good thing. (Psalm 34:10)
- He will provide for all our needs. (Matthew 6:24-33)
- He will reward those who believe in Him and trust Him. (Hebrews 11:6)

How do we seek and practice His presence? We are to seek Him in His Word and come before Him in prayer. We are to follow Him by obeying His Word. And we are to be diligent in this task—*beat a path, frequent this place, tread here.*

When we tread, we leave marks behind…tread marks. What are the tread marks in your life that are evidence you have been in the Lord's presence?

SHINE

Reflect on the verses from today and on the fact that God is your joy and when you seek Him you find not only the joy of His presence, but strength for your day. Are you leaving an impression for others to see the evidence of God's presence imprinted on your life?

27

Day 27 — Overwhelmed with Joy!

SOAK
The joy of the LORD is your strength. —Nehemiah 8:10b

As we end our week celebrating the joy of God's presence, read the story in Nehemiah of God's people who were overwhelmed with joy. It is a great moment! Read, be encouraged and enjoy life more in light of who God is.

Read Nehemiah 8:1-12.

After years in exile and captivity, the Israelites returned to Jerusalem. Under the leadership of Nehemiah they began to rebuild the city, first the wall and then the temple. Ezra was the chief priest who returned as shepherd to the people. We read in Ezra 7:10 that Ezra set his heart to the study and observance of the Law of the Lord and to teaching its decrees and laws in Israel. *Set his heart,* meaning he was *devoted* and *set his heart toward* this thing.

Have you *set your heart* toward the Word? Have you made a determined, intentional decision and commitment to be in God's Word daily?

In Nehemiah 8 we find the people gathering in sacred assembly at the Feast of Tabernacles (see Leviticus 23 for the background on this event). As Ezra stood above the people to read the Word of God, he was not only reading, but *making it clear and giving the meaning so that the people could understand what was being read.* The Word of God was written in Hebrew. But the people had been so long in captivity, and had so assimilated into that culture, they no longer spoke or understood Hebrew. So Ezra read the Word in Aramaic so they could understand.

We have the great advantage of the Holy Spirit as our personal teacher and instructor. He makes the truths of God's Word clear to us.

Do you begin your time in God's Word with a prayer for the Holy Spirit to be your teacher, making clear the truths of God's Word?

The people's next response is that of weeping. It had been so long since they had heard the Word of God that it was overwhelming to their souls and spirits. In verse 10, Nehemiah instructed them, *to not grieve, for the joy of the Lord is your strength.* The word for *grieve* here carries the idea of *mental and physical discomfort*. It was a grieving of their souls and spirits because they had not heard the Word of God in so long. They were spiritually starved and thirsty. The fresh, powerful, living, and active Word of God had pierced their very souls and their response was an emotion so overwhelming they could not contain it!

Have you ever felt the same way? Have you found yourself living in a dry and parched land spiritually and in need of God's Word? Quench your thirst today with the refreshing truths of God's Word!

The timing of this event is also important. We read that it was the seventh month when they gathered in this sacred assembly. When God brought His people into the Promised Land from captivity in Egypt after years of wandering in the wilderness, He established several feasts for them to observe. One, in particular, was to remind them of their delivery from captivity and the years God provided for them in the desert. The Israelites were now returning from years of captivity and wilderness-living once again. How divinely appropriate that God would choose this month to have Ezra read the Word to the people! The Feast of Tabernacles or Booths was an eight-day feast. The first and eighth days were to be a day of rest before the Lord with no work being performed. On days two through seven, the people were to offer sacrifices by fire and "rejoice in the Lord". This feast was observed at the end of the harvest, just after they gathered the crops. They were to decorate the "booths" or "tabernacles" with choice fruit from trees, with palm fronds, leafy branches, and poplars.

It was a time of celebration—they had been set free from captivity. They had worked hard to rebuild their city despite constant opposition and hardship. Now they were to celebrate and rejoice before the Lord! God uses the reading of His Word to begin this time of celebration. The very words of God spoken directly to their hearts to meet whatever their need was at that moment. Their greatest need was to be near, in fellowship and communion with their God!

We know that God established the tabernacle in the wilderness as a way and a place that He might dwell among His people. This is still His heart's desire

This is still our greatest need and greatest joy today. We don't have to wait for a yearly feast or event to meet with our God and experience His presence. In Christ Jesus, God meets us faithfully in whatever place or state we find ourselves because we have His Spirit living in us. He is always faithful and ever-present! So rejoice, be glad, and enjoy life more—in His presence!

Though the fig tree should not blossom,
nor fruit be on the vines,
the produce of the olive fail
and the fields yield no food,
the flock be cut off from the fold
and there be no herd in the stalls,
yet I will rejoice in the LORD;
I will take joy in the God of my salvation.
God, the LORD, is my strength;
he makes my feet like the deer's;
he makes me tread on my high places.
—Habakkuk 3:17-19

SHINE
Reflect on the verses from today and on the fact that God is your joy! Praise Him for meeting you at the point of your greatest need and for the joy of His presence which is your strength!

Day 28 — Reasons for Rejoicing!

SOAK
I will rejoice and be glad in your steadfast love, because you have seen my affliction; you have known the distress of my soul, and you have not delivered me into the hand of the enemy; you have set my feet in a broad place. —Psalm 31:7-8

Read Psalm 30:1-12. Let's close our week of focusing on God as our joy by rehearsing some of the reasons we have to rejoice.

Look at some of the reasons found in Psalm 30 that we have to rejoice in God's presence and what He has done for us:

- heals
- restores life to me from the pit
- gives favor for a lifetime
- my weeping lasts for the night, but joy comes in morning
- makes me stand strong
- turns my mourning into dancing
- clothes me with gladness

SHINE
Spend time praising God for being your reason to rejoice. Reflect on the reasons found in Psalm 30 and any others that come to mind

Summer Fireworks and Freedom

Fireworks are often part of our summer celebrations. We find ourselves *oohing and aahing* as the fireworks are shot high into the night air. We are captivated by their splendor and majestic display. Here in the United States, we celebrate our freedom on July 4th with grand displays of fireworks, parades, barbecues and music. Let's use the imagery of fireworks and our freedom celebrations to prompt us to praise God for His majesty and splendor, and for providing us with the greatest freedom of all—salvation in Jesus. Let's celebrate the freedom we experience as we live in complete abandon to the God who is limitless, our deliverer, our Savior, our provider and protector!

Day 29 — His Limitless, Infinite Majesty!

SOAK

Yours, O LORD, is the greatness and the power and the glory and the victory and the majesty, for all that is in the heavens and in the earth is yours. Yours is the kingdom, O LORD, and you are exalted as head above all. Both riches and honor come from you, and you rule over all. In your hand are power and might, and in your hand it is to make great and to give strength to all. —1 Chronicles 29:11-12

Our word for *majesty* comes from a Latin word meaning *greatness*. When the Scriptures speak of the majesty of God, it is always describing an aspect of God's greatness. Whenever we study God's Word and consider and contemplate God's greatness, it naturally brings us to a posture of worship.

How do we form a right idea of God's greatness? We begin by making much of God. We tend to limit God in our thoughts and minds. We make Him too small! When we compare God with powers and forces that are great, we begin to form a right idea of His greatness. Let's do that today as we read through two passages of Scripture.

Read Isaiah 40:25-27. Consider and answer for yourself the questions Isaiah poses in these verses.

Question #1: *To whom then will you compare me, that I should be like him? says the Holy One.* —Isaiah 40:25

What is God's response?

Lift up your eyes on high and see: who created these? He who brings out their host by number, calling them all by name, by the greatness of his might, and because he is strong in power not one is missing. —Isaiah 40:26

'Before me no god was formed, nor shall there be any after me. I, I am the Lord, and besides me there is no savior. I declared and saved and proclaimed, when there was no strange god among you; and you are my witnesses,' declares the Lord, 'and I am God. Also henceforth I am he; there is none who can deliver from my hand; I work, and who can turn it back?' —Isaiah 43:10b-13

For thus says the Lord, who created the heavens (he is God!), who formed the earth and made it (he established it; he did not create it empty, he formed it to be inhabited!): 'I am the Lord, and there is no other'. —Isaiah 45:18

Question #2: *Why do you say...'My way is hidden from the Lord, and my right is disregarded by my God'?* — Isaiah 40:27

What is God's response?

Have you not known? Have you not heard? The LORD is the everlasting God, the Creator of the ends of the earth. He does not faint or grow weary; his understanding is unsearchable. He gives power to the faint, and to him who has no might he increases strength. Even youths shall faint and be weary, and young men shall fall exhausted; but they who wait for the LORD shall renew their strength; they shall mount up with wings like eagles; they shall run and not be weary; they shall walk and not faint. — Isaiah 40:28-31

But now thus says the LORD, he who created you, O Jacob, he who formed you, O Israel: "Fear not, for I have redeemed you; I have called you by name, you are mine. When you pass through the waters, I will be with you; and through the rivers, they shall not overwhelm you; when you walk through fire you shall not be burned, and the flame shall not consume you. For I am the LORD your God, the Holy One of Israel, your Savior...Because you are precious in my eyes, and honored, and I love you...everyone who is called by my name, whom I created for my glory, whom I formed and made. —Isaiah 43:1-4,7

Let's close today by reading one other passage that speaks to the limitless and infinite majesty of our God. **Read Psalm 139.**

What were some ways the psalmist meditated on the infinite and unlimited nature of God's presence, knowledge, and power in relation to people? Record what you learn by completing the prompts below.

- His presence is....
- His knowledge is...
- His power is...
- His relationship with people is...

SHINE
How does the fact that God is infinite, limitless, great, awesome, powerful, and yet so very intimate with those who are His encourage you today? Reflect on the verses from today and on the fact that God is your freedom. He is without boundaries—limitless—yet so close and intimate to you through Christ Jesus!

Day 30—True Freedom!

SOAK

What is true freedom? How do we live lives that are truly marked by freedom, peace, and contentment? Today I want us to simply SOAK in the Word and be reminded and reassured of the foundation and source of our true freedom. Read slowly and let the truth of God's Word soak deep into your soul and spirit!

And I will live a life of freedom because I pursue Your precepts.
—Psalm 119:45 (The Voice)

Now the Lord is the Spirit, and where the Spirit of the Lord is, there is freedom. We all, with unveiled faces, are looking as in a mirror at the glory of the Lord and are being transformed into the same image from glory to glory; this is from the Lord who is the Spirit —2 Corinthians 3:17-18 (HCSB)

For while we were still helpless, at the appointed moment, Christ died for the ungodly. For rarely will someone die for a just person—though for a good person perhaps someone might even dare to die. But God proves His own love for us in that while we were still sinners, Christ died for us!
—Romans 5:6-8 (HCSB)

There is now no condemnation for those who are in Christ Jesus!
—Romans 8:1 (HCSB)

May you be strengthened with all power, according to His glorious might, for all endurance and patience, with joy giving thanks to the Father, who has enabled you to share in the saints' inheritance in the light. He has rescued us from the domain of darkness and transferred us into the kingdom of the Son He loves. We have redemption, the forgiveness of sins, in Him. —Colossians 1:11-14 (HCSB)

But God, who is rich in mercy, because of His great love that He had for us, made us alive with the Messiah even though we were dead in trespasses. You are saved by grace! Together with Christ Jesus He also raised us up and seated us in the heavens, so that in the coming ages He might display the immeasurable riches of His grace through His kindness to us in Christ Jesus. For you are saved by grace through faith, and this is not from yourselves; it is God's gift—not from works, so that no one can boast. For we are His creation, created in Christ Jesus for good works, which God prepared ahead of time so that we should walk in them.
—Ephesians 2:4-10 (HCSB)

SHINE
Reflect on the verses from today and on the fact that God is your freedom. In Christ Jesus you have been set free from the penalty and power of sin in your life! Give thanks to God for the victory Christ has provided you and the freedom you experience each day as you live surrendered to Him. Praise Him!

Day 31 — He is My Deliverer!

SOAK

There are days when we feel like we are being attacked at every turn. There are seasons when we are weary and battle-worn, hoping for some relief. Many times the enemies we face are not just from without but are within our own hearts and souls. Are you battling an enemy today? Could you use a deliverer?

I love you, O LORD, my strength. The Lord is my rock and my fortress and my deliverer, my God, my rock, in whom I take refuge, my shield, and the horn of my salvation, my stronghold. I call upon the LORD, who is worthy to be praised, and I am saved from my enemies. —Psalm 18:1-3

He sent from on high, he took me; he drew me out of many waters. He rescued me from my strong enemy and from those who hated me, for they were too mighty for me. They confronted me in the day of my calamity, but the LORD was my support. He brought me out into a broad place; he rescued me, because he delighted in me. —Psalm 18:16-19

I know in my own life one of the greatest enemies I am confronted with and battle on a daily basis is my own sin and selfishness. The Bible refers to it as "my flesh" (Romans 7-8). It is that part of me that is still affected by sin and a fallen world. In Christ Jesus I am a new creation with a redeemed heart and spirit that is alive to the ways and things of God. In Christ I have a new desire, motive, and passion to live in a way that pleases God. But because I am still clothed in this body of flesh, and living in a sinful and fallen world, I will still battle the flesh and its ways.

- My flesh lashes out in anger.
- My flesh is impatient with others when I'm in a hurry.
- My flesh yells at my children.
- My flesh sees interruptions as obstacles.
- My flesh seeks its own way.
- My flesh wants praise.

- My flesh complains about circumstances.
- My flesh is not grateful.
- My flesh likes to boast.
- My flesh criticizes others.
- My flesh judges others' weaknesses.
- My flesh always wants to be right.
- My flesh does not accept constructive criticism.
- My flesh is selfish.

We deal with our flesh and its desires on a daily basis in every aspect of our lives. The flesh is constantly ready to rear its ugly head and demand, "I deserve it my way" and "I have rights!"

I have been crucified with Christ. It is no longer I who live, but Christ who lives in me. And the life I now live in the flesh I live by faith in the Son of God, who loved me and gave himself for me. —Galatians 2:20

For to me to live is Christ, and to die is gain. —Philippians 1:21

According to Galatians 2:20 and Philippians 1:21, we are no longer to live for the flesh, but surrendered to Christ Jesus. There is no getting around that daily battle of dealing with our flesh. But we are not left without help. Jesus promised when He left earth that He would not leave His followers without help. God sent his Holy Spirit to indwell each of us who confess and believe upon the name of Jesus. Jesus is our help and deliverer every single day, in every single moment. Praise Him!

SHINE
Reflect on the verses from today and on the fact that God is your freedom. What attacks of the flesh are you battling today? Remember, in Christ Jesus you have been set free from the penalty and power of sin in your life! In Christ Jesus you are a new creation with a redeemed heart and spirit that is alive to the ways and things of God. Praise Him!

32

Day 32 — He is My Banner!

SOAK
...his banner over me was love. —Song of Solomon 2:4b

Read Exodus 17:1-16.

We first encounter the name of God, *Jehovah Nissi,* in the book of Exodus (Exodus 17:1-16). The people find themselves fighting a great enemy, one that just keeps coming. After the battle with Amalek, Moses builds an altar and calls it *Jehovah Nissi, The Lord is my banner.* In the Old Testament a banner generally meant a rallying point or standard, which drew people together for some common action or for the communication of important information. This usually happened on a high or conspicuous place within the community. A signal pole, sometimes with an ensign attached, could be raised as a point of focus or object of hope.

A banner is a wonderful picture of God's protection and deliverance. His banner over us symbolizes His presence, His power and His provision. God as our banner is a symbol and reminder that we need to depend on God for victory in our battles and not our own strength and effort.

We've talked a little about battles this week. Many scholars see Amalek as a picture representing the enemies that God's people face—those enemies being the flesh, the world and the devil (Galatians 5:16, John 16:33, Galatians 6:14, 1 Peter 5:8-10). But like the Israelites, when we face an enemy we are not called to fight in our own strength and power. We are to trust and know that the Lord will fight for us. We are to rely upon Him. We are to look to Jesus—our Banner, *Jehovah Nissi*!

*In that day the root of Jesse, who shall stand as a signal for the peoples—
of him shall the nations inquire, and his resting place shall be glorious.*
—Isaiah 11:10. The root of Jesse is a reference to Christ.

*No, in all these things we are more than conquerors through him who
loved us. For I am sure that neither death nor life, nor angels nor rulers,
nor things present nor things to come, nor powers, nor height nor depth,
nor anything else in all creation, will be able to separate us from the love
of God in Christ Jesus our Lord.* —Romans 8:37-39

*You have set up a banner for those who fear you, that they may flee to it
from the bow. Selah.* —Psalm 60:4

*Some trust in chariots and some in horses, but we trust in the name of the
Lord our God. They collapse and fall, but we rise and stand upright.*
—Psalm 20:7-8

It is easy to become discouraged when we look at the world and the daily
suffering and discord we see around us. It is easy to become discouraged
and feel defeated in our own lives at times. But I love what Hebrews
teaches us! The book of Hebrews begins with the author reminding us of
how God speaks to us.

Read Hebrews 1:1-3 and note how God spoke in the past and how He
speaks now.

In these last days, God has spoken to us through His Son! The author then
goes on to exclaim and expound about the greatness and superiority of
Jesus and the fact that one day, Jesus will return and rule and reign over
all. (Hebrews 2:5-10) As a matter of fact, the entire book of Hebrews is all
about how Jesus is better, superior to anything and everything. He is
greater than anything we are tempted to trust in this life. But I really love
Hebrews 2:8-9:

*At present, we do not yet see everything in subjection to him. But we see
him who for a little while was made lower than the angels, namely Jesus,
crowned with glory and honor because of the suffering of death, so that by
the grace of God he might taste death for everyone.* —Hebrews 2:8b-9

Did you catch that? *At present,* we don't see everything in subjection to Jesus. It may appear at times as if the world (and perhaps your life) is spinning out of control. But we have this hope as an anchor for our souls. But we see Him, namely Jesus! He is our banner. He is the One we are to look to as our focal point, our object of hope. (Hebrews 6:19) His banner over me is love! He is my victory, my banner, in the midst of the battles of life.

SHINE
Reflect on the verses from today and on the fact that God is majestic and holy and His banner over you is love. Praise Jesus as your deliverer, Jehovah-Nissi. He is your victory in the midst of the battles of life!

33

Day 33 — Celebrate His Majesty!

SOAK
Splendor and majesty are before him; strength and joy are in his place.
—1 Chronicles 16:27

Read through Psalm 93 today and make a list of the characteristics of God—who He is and what He does.

What do you learn about who God is and what He does?

How does this encourage you today?

The LORD reigns! He is robed in majesty; The LORD is robed, enveloped in strength. The world is firmly established; it cannot be shaken. Your throne has been established from the beginning; You are from eternity. The floods have lifted up, LORD, the floods have lifted up their voice; the floods lift up their pounding waves. Greater than the roar of many waters—the mighty breakers of the sea—the LORD on high is majestic. LORD, Your testimonies are completely reliable; holiness is the beauty of Your house for all the days to come. —Psalm 93:1-5 (HCSB)

SHINE
Praise God by praying Psalm 93 back to Him. Go verse by verse, proclaiming who God is and what He does. Make it personal. Pray it in light of whatever you are facing today. Pray it in light of whatever is weighing heavy on your heart today. Reflect on the verses from today and on the fact that God is majestic and glorious!

Day 34 — He is Holy!

SOAK
Bless the LORD, O my soul, and all that is within me, bless his holy name!
—Psalm 103:1

Read Psalm 103:1-22. List the benefits for which the psalmist expresses gratitude in this verse. What do these verses reveal about God? How should we respond to God?

Read Ephesians 1:3-11. List the many ways God blesses us in Christ Jesus.

SHINE
Reflect on the verses from today. Make a list of the things for which you are grateful. List the things that come to mind easily and make you feel good. But I challenge and encourage you to list the things for which it is difficult to give thanks. Praise your God who is majestic and holy and who has blessed you with every spiritual blessing in the heavenly realms!

35

Day 35 — The Spirit of Freedom

SOAK

This week we have contemplated and praised our God who is majestic and holy, our Deliverer, *Jehovah-Nissi* (our Banner); the source of true freedom in our lives.

In the United States on July 4th, we celebrate our freedom and remember and give thanks for those who have served sacrificially and faithfully to protect those freedoms for us. This desire to serve others should characterize our lives as those who can rejoice and celebrate our freedom in Christ.

Now the Lord is the Spirit, and where the Spirit of the Lord is, there is freedom. And we all, with unveiled face, beholding the glory of the Lord, are being transformed into the same image from one degree of glory to another. For this comes from the Lord who is the Spirit. —2 Corinthians 3:17-18

Where the Spirit of the Lord is, there is freedom. We walk in freedom because of who we are in Christ and what He has done to set us free from sin and death. We experience the joy and peace of true freedom as God's Word and Spirit daily transform our lives—our thoughts, our behaviors and our attitudes—so that we respond more like Jesus. As God changes us from the inside out, it brings about a desire to love and serve Him, and to love and serve others. (Matthew 22:36-39)

For freedom Christ has set us free; stand firm therefore, and do not submit again to a yoke of slavery...For you were called to freedom, brothers. Only do not use your freedom as an opportunity for the flesh, but through love serve one another. —Galatians 5:1, 13

Loving and serving others is not always easy and does not come naturally to us. It requires us to seek, rely upon, and look to Jesus for the strength and power needed to serve and love others as He does. As our theme for this devotion expresses, we SOAK in God's Word and His presence so that we might pour out and SHINE, reflecting Jesus to others, all to the praise and glory of God!

SHINE
Reflect on the verses from today and on the fact that God is majestic and holy, your Deliverer, your Freedom! How might God be calling you to use your freedom in Christ to serve and love someone today?

Lazy Summer Days on the Porch

I love a porch in the summertime. I have an entire Pinterest board devoted to my "some day" dream porch. I love sitting in the swing, rocking in the rocking chair, relaxing with a good book and glass of iced tea or gathering with friends and family for good food, conversation and laughter. The porch is a great place to relax, unwind, put your feet up and take a load off at the end of your day. It is a comfortable and peaceful place. This week, let's use the imagery of the front porch to prompt us to praise God who is our comfort, our peace, our burden-bearer and the One to whom we can run for refuge any time we need. (Hebrews 4:16)

Day 36 — He is My Burden-Bearer

SOAK

May the Lord be praised! Day after day He bears our burdens; God is our salvation. Selah—Psalm 68:19 (HCSB)

This is one of my favorite "front porch" kind of verses. It is one of those great reminders to me at the end of a long day (or season) when my heart is heavy with the burdens and cares of this life. It is like that swing on the front porch where I can sit, take a load off, and let the rhythm relax my body and mind. God is my burden-bearer. I can take my cares before Him, pour out my heart to Him and leave it all in His hands. And the wonderful thing is I can do this anytime I need—over and over and over again. Because I know at some point I'll try to pick it up again. I'll try to shoulder it all and fix it all. I love that He is always there, ever-present, ready to hear my heart, bear my burden and flood my heart and soul with His peace.

I love how this verse ends—*Selah*. Selah is a musical term found often in the psalms. It is a word of undetermined meaning, but is believed to convey a pause, interlude or interruption. Some believe it is a statement of fact, "let it be so." I think of it as a long sigh—an exhale— where we let it all go and lay it at the Savior's feet. It is that much-needed interruption and pause in all our busyness, "fixing", fretting, and weariness where we stop and lay our burdens down.

Hear God's heart in a cross-reference verse for Psalm 68:19:

Even to your old age I am he, and to gray hairs I will carry you. I have made, and I will bear; I will carry and will save. —Isaiah 46:4

Praise be to the Lord, to God, my Savior, who daily bears my burdens!

SHINE

Reflect on the verses from today and on the fact that God is your burden-bearer! What's burdening your heart today? Exhale and let it go. Lay it at the Savior's feet. Let the Lord be your burden-bearer and walk in His peace and comfort today.

37

Day 37 — His Comfort Brings Joy!

SOAK
When I am filled with cares, Your comfort brings me joy. —Psalm 94:19
(HCSB)

When the cares of my heart are many, your consolations cheer my soul.
—Psalm 94:19 (ESV)

In the original language, the word, *cares,* in this verse means *disquieting
thoughts, divided in mind.* Cares. I have them and they often weigh my
heart and soul down leaving me feeling defeated, discouraged and
distraught.

Are you having one of those days or seasons of life when the cares of your
heart are many? Perhaps your heart, soul and mind are weighed down
with disquieting thoughts that are distracting and consuming you.

I love how the Word of God meets us right where we are, in the midst of
our everyday moments, further solidifying what Hebrews 4:12 teaches us;
God's Word is living and active! It is living, breathing, fresh, powerful, and
effective. This is exactly what Psalm 94:19 did for me one heavy-hearted
day.

Psalm 94:19 reminded me that God's *comfort* brings joy and cheer to my
soul when I'm filled with care. This word in the original language simply
means that God *takes something bad and makes it better.*

I don't have to carry the burdens that are weighing my heart and soul
down. I can exchange them for the joy and peace that God's presence
brings. This simply involves telling God how I'm feeling, what I'm thinking,
what's on my mind, and those things burdening my heart and soul. It is a
conversation. That's what prayer is—a conversation with God. Often it is
just being able to "get it out", to verbalize, and process all that is going on
in my heart and head. And the Father listens! I love the word picture that

85

Psalm 116:2 gives when it tells us that God *bends down to hear* me. He is a faithful Father who never tires of hearing from His children. He longs for us to come to Him and *pour out our hearts* to Him. (Psalm 62:8)

If we read Psalm 94 in its entirety, we see some of the ways the Father's comfort will cheer our souls:

For the LORD will not forsake his people... Psalm 94:14

He is our help... Psalm 94:17

His steadfast love upholds us... Psalm 94:18

He is our stronghold and rock of refuge... Psalm 94:22

SHINE
If the cares of your heart are many today, unburden your heart and soul. Run to the One who is your rock of refuge, your stronghold, your help, the One who upholds you, and will never forsake you. Exchange your cares for the comfort of His presence. Reflect on the verses from today and on the fact that God is your Comforter. Imagine sitting in a rocker on the front porch telling the Lord all that is on your heart and mind.

Day 38 — He is My Comfort!

SOAK

Life hurts sometimes. We all face times of loss, disappointment, hardship, discouragement and doubt. Where do you turn for comfort?

Praise the God and Father of our Lord Jesus Christ, the Father of mercies and the God of all comfort. He comforts us in all our affliction, so that we may be able to comfort those who are in any kind of affliction, through the comfort we ourselves receive from God. —2 Corinthians 1:3-4 (HCSB)

Read how Paul describes his situation in his letter to the Corinthians: *For we do not want you to be unaware, brothers, of the affliction we experienced in Asia. For we were so utterly burdened beyond our strength that we despaired of life itself. Indeed, we felt that we had received the sentence of death.* —2 Corinthians 1:8-9

Can you relate to any of these? Burdened beyond your strength? Despair? But if you read on, Paul gives us a proper perspective to adopt in the midst of being burdened and in times hardship:

But that was to make us rely not on ourselves but on God who raises the dead. He delivered us from such a deadly peril, and he will deliver us. On him we have set our hope that he will deliver us again. —2 Corinthians 1:9-10

We have hope! As painful or uncomfortable as these situations may be they serve to teach us to rely on God and run to Him as our Comforter. We read in this verse that **God delivered**, **will deliver,** and **will deliver us again.** That's good news!

Too often my idea of deliverance from something painful or difficult is different from what is promised in this verse. The word for *deliver* in the original language means *to draw to one's self, to rescue.* I often want the deliverance to be *out of* or the *end to* a circumstance. I just want the pain to go away! But God delivers by drawing me to Himself. He is my place of refuge, security, hope, peace, and joy in the midst of hardship and trial. Because...He IS hope. He IS peace. He IS joy. He IS steadfast and immovable. He IS the true source of these things in my life and they are not dependent upon my circumstances.

This week we have praised God as our burden-bearer. But this passage also confirms that we need each other in the difficult times in our lives. Look at our verse for today again:

Blessed be the God and Father of our Lord Jesus Christ, the Father of mercies and God of all comfort, who comforts us in all our affliction, so that we may be able to comfort those who are in any affliction, with the comfort with which we ourselves are comforted by God.
—2 Corinthians 1:3-4

Because God bears our burdens and is our Comforter, in turn we are called to come alongside others to help bear their burdens, encouraging them as they walk through times of hardship, heartache, and difficulty. In fact, the word *comfort* used in 2 Corinthians means *a calling near, to encourage, console, and comfort.* We comfort as we come alongside to encourage through a listening ear, a word of Scripture, a hug, a prayer, a helping hand, a shoulder to cry on, and a heart that sympathizes instead of judges.

Bear one another's burdens, and so fulfill the law of Christ. —Galatians 6:2

We don't have to do this in our own strength because the God of All Comfort is our source of comfort and as He has comforted us, by His presence and Spirit, we are able to comfort others.

SHINE
Reflect on the verses from today. God is your Comforter. How has God comforted you? How might you use your experience to extend comfort and love to another? Is there someone Christ is calling you to encourage, to come alongside and comfort today?

Day 39 — He is My Peace

SOAK

Peace. It is something we all long for and seek. When we search for peace in the things of the world, we will become frustrated and disappointed. But we can experience peace in this world, even amidst conflict and turmoil.

Peace is defined as *a state in which there is no war or fighting; a state of tranquility or quiet: as freedom from civil disturbance; a state of security or order within a community provided for by law or custom; freedom from disquieting or oppressive thoughts or emotions; harmony in personal relations. (Merriam-Webster)*

Our true source of lasting peace is found in God's presence, because He IS peace! In the Old Testament, one of the names of God we discover is *Jehovah Shalom,* meaning *the Lord is Peace. Shalom* in the original language means *completeness, soundness, safety, quiet, tranquility, contentment.*

In the New Testament the word for *peace* means *a state of national tranquility; peace between individuals, security, safety; metaphorically, peace of mind, tranquility arising from reconciliation with God and a sense of divine favor; the tranquil state of a soul assured of its salvation through Christ, and so fearing nothing from God and content with its earthly lot, of whatsoever sort that is. (Complete Word Study Bible Dictionary)*

God's Word confirms that fixing and focusing our minds upon the truths of Scripture are key to experiencing peace in our lives. When we rehearse God's Word, we are affirming and reminding ourselves of who He is. His presence is our peace.

SHINE

Take a few moments to soak in the truth of God's Word. Below you will find several Scripture verses on peace. Read slowly. Stop and ponder the verse after you read it. Allow God's truth to wash over you and flood your heart and soul with His presence and peace. As you read the verses, note the connection between your trust in God and your experiencing peace. They are always connected. *Now may the Lord of peace himself give you peace at all times in every way. The Lord be with you all.* (2 Thessalonians 3:16)

You keep him in perfect peace whose mind is stayed on you, because he trusts in you. —Isaiah 26:3

May the LORD give strength to his people! May the LORD bless his people with peace! —Psalm 29:11

And the effect of righteousness will be peace, and the result of righteousness, quietness and trust forever. My people will abide in a peaceful habitation, in secure dwellings, and in quiet resting places. —Isaiah 32:17-18

I have said these things to you, that in me you may have peace. In the world you will have tribulation. But take heart; I have overcome the world. —John 16:33

Do not be anxious about anything, but in everything by prayer and supplication with thanksgiving let your requests be made known to God. And the peace of God, which surpasses all understanding, will guard your hearts and your minds in Christ Jesus. Finally, brothers, whatever is true, whatever is honorable, whatever is just, whatever is pure, whatever is lovely, whatever is commendable, if there is any excellence, if there is anything worthy of praise, think about these things. What you have learned and received and heard and seen in me practice these things, and the God of peace will be with you. —Philippians 4:6-9

Further Scriptures on peace: Psalm 119:165, Isaiah 9:6, Isaiah 54:10, John 14:27, Romans 5:1, Romans 8:6, Romans 15:13, Galatians 5:22, Ephesians 2:13-14, James 3:17-18.

Day 40 — He is the Lifter of My Head

SOAK
But You, LORD, are a shield around me, my glory, and the One who lifts up my head. —Psalm 3:3 (HCSB)

Do you ever have those days when you're just having the blahs? Those days where you're weighed down with a heaviness of your heart and spirit? I know I do. Sometimes it is because I've got too much on my mind and too much in my schedule for the day. Sometimes it is because life is hard and relationships are messy. Sometimes it is because I'm burdened by the circumstance or heartache that someone I know is experiencing. And sometimes...I just have the blahs for no apparent reason. During these times I have a choice. I can give into the blah and go about my day with my head down and feet dragging or I can turn to the One who is the lifter of my head!

Read Psalm 3.
The psalmist is having one of those days. His foes are rising up against him. He's feeling weary and despised. He's fearful. But quickly the psalmist turns his eyes to the Lord. He declares who God is. He cries out to the Lord and God answers him.

God responds, reassuring and encouraging him that:
- He is a shield about him.
- He is his glory.
- He is the lifter of his head.
- He listens.
- He grants him sleep.
- He sustains. I love this word picture it means to lean against or lay upon, rest upon.
- He saves.
- He defends and fights for him.
- He blesses.

The psalmist praises God as his shield, his protector and defender, his glory, the One who gives his life true worth and meaning, the Lifter of his head.

I love the word picture of God being the Lifter of my head! During those times when we are discouraged and feeling defeated, this is just what we need. We need someone to stand beside us, someone to lean against, someone to protect and defend us, and someone to remind us where we find our true worth and purpose in life. The Lifter of my head changes my perspective from an inward and downward gaze to an upward one. My focus is set on the Lord—who He is and what He has done—and this lifts my head and my heart!

SHINE
What is causing you to walk around heavy-hearted and discouraged today? Look up! Look to Jesus. Find a renewed sense of joy, peace, and perspective. Reflect on the verses from today and on the fact that God is your Peace, your Comforter, and the Lifter of your head. Make this your prayer, *Father God, I praise you because you are a shield around me, O Lord; you bestow glory on me and lift up my head when I am weary or despised.*

Day 41 — He is My Resting Place!

SOAK

Our summer days are winding down. Perhaps you're finding yourself a bit worn and weary. Maybe you've had a busy summer or perhaps life has just been overwhelming in general. Could you use some rest? I've got the perfect spot! Let's sit a spell on the front porch this week.

Come to me all you who are weary and burdened, and I will give you rest...and you will find rest for your souls. —Matthew 11:28-29 (NIV)

Look at the definitions in the original language for this verse:

Weary – *fatigued, worn out, weary and faint*. It is a word used to denote not so much the actual exertion we experience in labor, but the weariness experience from that labor.

Burdened – *a word meaning the freight of a ship, to be overloaded or heavily burdened.*

Rest – *to refresh; to cause one to cease from any movement or labor in order to recover and collect his strength; to give rest, to keep quiet, of calm and patient expectation.*

Find Rest – *intermission; rest while performing necessary labor*. It describes the inner peace and tranquility, the rest of the soul even in the midst of difficult circumstances.

What a great place to find the rest we need...

- When we are worn out, fatigued and weary.
- When we are overloaded and heavily burdened.
- When we need to be refreshed and to recover our strength.
- When we need rest, even in the midst of our work.
- When we need rest in the midst of difficult circumstances.

Rest in...

- God's unfailing love. (Zephaniah 3:17)
- God's faithfulness and mercy. (Lamentations 3:22-24)
- God's purpose and plans for you. (Psalm 57:2-3, Romans 8:28-32)
- God's strength. (Psalm 28:7, Psalm 73:26)
- God's presence. (Psalm 139:1-14)
- God's peace. (Psalm 29:11, John 14:27)
- God's power. (Psalm 55:22, 2 Corinthians 12:9-10)

Jesus beckons us to come and find rest!

- Come to Him as you read and reflect upon His powerful and energizing Word.
- Come to Him in prayer as you lift your burdens to Him and leave them in His care.
- Come to Him as you confess your sins and receive His forgiveness and peace.
- Come to Him with praise and adoration, regardless of the situation, simply because of who He is.
- Come to Him seeking His wisdom, comfort, love, security, rest and renewal.

SHINE

Reflect on the verses from today and on the fact that God is your peace and rest. Come to Jesus, pour out your heart to Him, and find rest.

42

Day 42 — Peace & Provision in His Presence

SOAK

Let's end our week praising God who is our Peace, our Comforter, our Burden-Bearer and our Rest, by focusing on a beautiful and familiar Psalm.

Psalm 23 is probably very familiar to most of us. I love to read a familiar passage in several translations of Scripture. It brings a freshness to the passage. Take a moment to read this psalm in a Bible translation that is different from what you normally use. Read slowly. Each time the psalmist mentions what the Lord does for him, pause and reflect upon this in your own life. Pray the psalm back to the Lord. Let God's Word soak into your soul and spirit, renewing your heart and mind!

The LORD is my shepherd; I shall not want.
He makes me lie down in green pastures.
He leads me beside still waters.
He restores my soul.
He leads me in paths of righteousness
for his name's sake.
Even though I walk through the valley of the shadow of death,
I will fear no evil,
for you are with me;
your rod and your staff,
they comfort me.
You prepare a table before me
in the presence of my enemies;
you anoint my head with oil;
my cup overflows.
Surely goodness and mercy shall follow me
all the days of my life,
and I shall dwell in the house of the Lord
forever. —Psalm 23

God is our Good Shepherd and He meets our every need. In this psalm we see that He provides nourishment and refreshment, restoration, guidance and protection. In John 10 we read that Jesus is our Good Shepherd. I love how the "I AM" names and attributes of God in the Old Testament are completely and eternally fulfilled in Jesus!

The thief comes only to steal and kill and destroy. I came that they may have life and have it abundantly. I am the good shepherd. The good shepherd lays down his life for the sheep. —John 10:10-11

I am the good shepherd. I know my own and my own know me, just as the Father knows me and I know the Father; and I lay down my life for the sheep. —John 10:14-15

SHINE
Reflect on the verses from today and on the fact that God is your Peace and Comforter. What is your greatest need today? Rest at the feet of the Good Shepherd today and allow Him to meet your every need!

Further "I AM" names of Jesus to read and reflect upon:
I am. —John 8:58
I am the bread of life. —John 6:35, 48, 51
I am the light of the world. —John 8:12; 9:5
I am the door of the sheep. —John 10:7, 9
I am the good shepherd. —John 10:11, 14
I am the resurrection and the life. — John 11:25
I am the way, the truth and the life. —John 14:6
I am the true vine. —John 15:1
I am the alpha and the omega, the beginning and the end, the first and the last. —Revelation 22:13

Fleeting Summer Days

As sure as summer days arrive, we know that they will come to an end. Schedules are about to shift as children head back to school and warm summer nights give way to chilly autumn breezes. It is my prayer that as you've used the imagery of summer to remind you to praise the Lord, you've known and experienced a deeper awareness of God's presence in your life. Let's close by focusing on the faithfulness of God. Unlike the changing seasons, He is ever-present, always faithful, sure, and steadfast.

Day 43 — He is Faithful!

SOAK

The steadfast love of the LORD never ceases; his mercies never come to an end; they are new every morning; great is your faithfulness.
—Lamentations 3:22-23

Be exalted, O God, above the heavens! Let your glory be over all the earth!
—Psalm 57:10-11

How is God's faithfulness described in these verses?
The definition for *faithfulness* in the original language means *stability, certainty, reliable, sureness, security* and *truth.* In a world that is often unreliable, uncertain, insecure, and lacking truth it is comforting and encouraging to know there is One who is faithful, unchanging, and always true!

Sometimes we miss the faithfulness of God in our lives because we are so self-sufficient and independent. But when we come to the end of ourselves—*to the end of our resources and our strength*—we see God's faithfulness so clearly. God is ever-faithful. He is always acting on our behalf, to love and care for us, to meet our every need, and sustain us in the dark and difficult times. He is faithful. He is reliable, sure, trustworthy, and true!

SHINE
Praise God for His faithfulness—His love, care, provision and protection. Take a moment to list the ways God has loved, cared for, provided for, and protected you. Be intentional to look for His faithfulness on a daily basis. Remember His greatest act of faithful love toward you is seen in what Jesus has done for you. He has restored and forgiven. He has brought you hope and eternal life.

Day 44 — Evidence of God's Faithfulness

SOAK

Know therefore that the LORD your God is God, the faithful God...
—Deuteronomy 7:9

What evidence do we have of God's faithfulness towards us?

God's faithfulness...

Is seen in His love towards us.
He reaches down from heaven and saves me, challenging the one who tramples me. Selah. God sends His faithful love and truth. —Psalm 57:3 (HCSB)

But God, who is rich in mercy, because of His great love that He had for us, made us alive with the Messiah even though we were dead in trespasses. You are saved by grace! —Ephesians 2:4-5 (HCSB)

Is seen in His word.
Your word, LORD, is eternal; it stands firm in the heavens. —Psalm 119:89 (NIV)

Is eternal.
Your faithfulness continues through all generations. —Psalm 119:90 (NIV)

Is seen in His works.
The works of his hands are faithful and just. —Psalm 111:7

Is not dependent upon our faithfulness.
If we are faithless, he will remain faithful for he cannot deny himself.
—2 Timothy 2:13

Is seen in His reconciling us and restoring us into a relationship with Him.
God is faithful; you were called by Him into fellowship with His Son, Jesus Christ our Lord. —1 Corinthians 1:9 (HCSB)

Is seen in His forgiveness of our sins.
If we confess our sins, he is faithful and just to forgive us our sins and to cleanse us from all unrighteousness. —1 John 1:9

Is seen in His protection over us from the enemy's attacks and temptation to sin.
But the Lord is faithful. He will establish you and guard you against the evil one. —2 Thessalonians 3:3

God is faithful, and He will not allow you to be tempted beyond what you are able, but with the temptation He will also provide a way of escape so that you are able to bear it. —1 Corinthians 10:13 (HCSB)

Is something we can count on in our daily walk and when we get discouraged.
Being confident of this, that he who began a good work in you will carry it on to completion until the day of Christ Jesus. —Philippians 1:6 (NIV)

Is an assurance that He is making us more like Jesus.
Now may the God of peace himself sanctify you completely, and may your whole spirit and soul and body be kept blameless at the coming of our Lord Jesus Christ. The one who calls you is faithful and he will do it. —1 Thessalonians 5:23-24

Is our encouragement to persevere in suffering.
Therefore let those who suffer according to God's will entrust their souls to a faithful Creator while doing good. —1 Peter 4:19

Is our assurance of a future inheritance and eternal life.
Let us hold fast the confession of our hope without wavering, for he who promised is faithful. —Hebrews 10:23

SHINE

What evidence of God's faithfulness do you see in your life? Reflect on the verses from today. Praise God today for His limitless and abundant faithfulness to you!

My lips will glorify You because Your faithful love is better than life.
—Psalm 63:3 (HCSB)

Day 45 — Great is His Faithfulness!

SOAK

Because of the LORD's faithful love we do not perish, for His mercies never end. They are new every morning; great is Your faithfulness!
—Lamentations 3:22-23 (HCSB)

Remembering God's faithfulness in the past helps us trust Him in the here and now. God's mercies never end and they are new to us each morning. When we feel overwhelmed, forgotten or frustrated with our circumstances in the present, it is comforting to remember God's faithfulness toward us in the past. Rehearsing who God is and what He has done for us builds our faith, lifts us above our present, and encourages us to trust Him with whatever each new day holds.

SHINE

Spend some time today rehearsing God's faithfulness in your life. It is helpful to journal or make a list. Use your list to praise God for who He is and His faithfulness toward you each and every moment of the day. His mercies never end, they are new each morning—great is His faithfulness!

Day 46 — When Praise and Faithfulness are Hard!

SOAK
Jesus Christ is the same yesterday and today and forever. —Hebrews 13:8

As I contemplate God's faithfulness and greatness, it also serves to magnify how often I am unfaithful in my walk with God. Faith is simply taking God at His Word, trusting Him, and walking that out in my life.

I often make promises I don't keep. I let circumstances overwhelm me and allow them to motivate my actions instead of trusting God. I get caught up in what's "fair" and "unfair" and my perspective turns inward instead of upward. The idols of my heart are many and my faithfulness is so shallow at times.

And trust is hard! We've all been hurt by another—betrayal, unfaithfulness, and abandonment are all too common in our world. We often respond by isolating and protecting ourselves, refusing to trust another. But this armadillo-shell lifestyle was never God's intention. We need one another, but more importantly, we need Him. Life is so much greater and full when we allow Him to heal those broken and empty places in our hearts and lives left by another—or by our own sin. God is so very faithful. We find completeness and wholeness in Jesus. (Colossians 2:10)

God understands our hearts and is not surprised by our faithlessness. His heart's cry is that we would be found faithful in our walk, but He knows this is impossible for us to do apart from Jesus and yielding to His Spirit at work in us. He addresses this very issue in His Word.

If we are faithless, he remains faithful—for he cannot deny himself.
—2 Timothy 2:13

And those who know your name put their trust in you, for you, O LORD, have not forsaken those who seek you. —Psalm 9:10

Jesus Christ is the same yesterday and today and forever. —Hebrews 13:8

God encourages and instructs us to continually offer up a "sacrifice" of praise to Him through Jesus. The answers to our faithlessness are always found in Jesus.

Through him [Jesus] *then let us continually offer up a sacrifice of praise to God, that is, the fruit of lips that acknowledge his name.* —Hebrews 13:15

I am so very thankful for the grace and faithfulness of God who understands the human heart and remains faithful to me—even though I am often unfaithful. We can trust the Lord because He is faithful and trustworthy!

SHINE
What is challenging your walk of faith today? Where do you need to offer a sacrifice of praise to God in Christ Jesus? In what areas of your life do you need to trust God and allow Him to heal and restore your broken and empty heart? You can trust Him to meet you where you are because He is so very faithful! Reflect on the verses from today and on the fact that God is faithful. Share with someone today how God has been faithful in your life. Great is His faithfulness!

Day 47 — A Praise Chat!

SOAK
Praise should continually be upon our lips. Our guiding verse for this devotion, Psalm 113:3, declares *from the rising of the sun to its setting, the name of the Lord is to be praised!*

Join me today for a praise chat.

Great is the LORD, and greatly to be praised, and his greatness is unsearchable. —Psalm 145:3

My mouth is full of praise and honor to You all day long. —Psalm 71:8 (HCSB)

There are many words for *praise* in the original language of both the Old and New Testaments.
Old Testament:
- *Halal* – to shine forth light, to be radiant, to be bright, to boast, celebrate, to glorify.
- *Yadah* – to throw, cast, shoot, to confess, to give thanks, praise.
- *Towdah* – confession, praise, thanksgiving, a hymn of praise.
- *Zamar* – to sing praise, to make music.
- *Mahalal* – to boast, to praise.
- *Hilluwl* – rejoicing praise; comes from the root word *halal*.
- *Shabach* – to address in a loud voice, to glorify, praise or adore God; to soothe or still with praises.

New Testament:
- *Ainos* – a praise or laudatory discourse, a story of praise
- *Ainesis* – a praise or thank offering
- *Doxa* – to think, to recognize, to glory; of honor due or rendered.
- *Epaineo* – to praise, to bestow praise upon, applaud, commend.
- *Eulogeo* – to praise, to celebrate with praise, to speak praise.
- *Hymneo* – to celebrate or praise in song.

We see that our praise can be a song, a story or an offering. It involves confession, thanksgiving, boasting and celebrating—all directed to our awesome God who is Creator, Almighty, Everlasting, Loving, Faithful, Merciful, Patient, Eternal and Holy. He is indescribable and therefore our praise knows no end!

Doxa, one of the New Testament words for ***praise,*** means *to glory.* It is the idea of *giving recognition to someone or something. It is the true appreciation of something's worth*. Glory is the true apprehension of God or things. Giving glory to God is ascribing to Him His full recognition.

What receives the greatest attention or recognition in your life as being of great worth and value to you?

Our lives should be a *story of praise* telling the world what God has done for us and in us. This world and the events of each day hold many distractions that can keep us from praise.

This is one reason I find it so valuable to note and study God's character, names, and attributes as I read my Bible. It is a way for me to remain aware and be intentional with focused attention in spite of the daily distractions.

Halal, one of the Old Testament words for *praise* means *to praise, to shine forth light, to be bright, to boast, to celebrate, to glorify*. At the heart of this root word is the idea of radiance. The well-known imperative phrase in the Hebrew *hallelujah* called for giving glory to God. Psalms 113-118 and Psalm 136 are known as the *hallel* psalms. These were psalms that were sung during special feasts such as, Passover, Pentecost and the Feast of Tabernacles. Psalm 136 is referred to as the *great hallel*. The structure of Psalm 136 uses the refrain, *His love endures forever,* after each stanza. This was possibly done in the format of responsive worship.

The word for *love* in Psalm 136 refers to God's unfailing love. Do you remember how multi-faceted God's unfailing love is? Psalm 136 expresses it so beautifully. As the psalmist declares an attribute of God, who He is or what He has done, it is followed with the response, *His love endures forever!*.

SHINE

For your praise time today, write your own *hallel*. Reflect on all that God has done for you, write it out, and then pray it back to the Lord. Consider using the format of the *great hallel* found in Psalm 136.

I will bless the LORD at all times; his praise shall continually be in my mouth. My soul makes its boast in the LORD; let the humble hear and be glad. Oh, magnify the LORD with me, and let us exalt his name together!
—Psalm 34:1-3

Day 48 — Faithful Beyond Comprehension!

SOAK
LORD God of Hosts, who is strong like You, LORD? Your faithfulness surrounds You. —Psalm 89:8 (HCSB)

Today be encouraged by the fact that God IS:

Omniscient—He is all-knowing.
He knows everything. (1 John 3:19-20, 1 Samuel 2:3)
His understanding has no limit. (Psalm 147:5)
He knows the minutest details of our lives. (Matthew 10:29-30)
He knows our thoughts before we speak them. (Psalm 139:4)
He has known us from eternity, even before we were created. (Psalm 139:1-3)
He knows all that will happen to the end of time. (Isaiah 46:9-10)
His knowledge is beyond our comprehension. (Isaiah 55:9)

Omnipresent—He is all-present, everywhere.
He is present in all time and space, but not limited to any time or space. (Psalm 139:8)
He fills all things with His presence. (Colossians 1:17)
He is always with us. We cannot hide from His presence. (Psalm 139:11-12, Hebrews 4:13)
He is ever present in our time of need. (Psalm 46:1, Hebrews 4:16)

Omnipotent—He is all-powerful.
He has power over all things, at all times, in all ways. (Job 42:1-2)
He is able to do immeasurably more than all we ask or imagine. (Ephesians 3:20)
His power cannot be thwarted. (Isaiah 43:11-13, Isaiah 14:27)
His power knows no limitations. Nothing is impossible for Him. (Luke 1:37)
His power is exalted in us when we are most weak. (2 Corinthians 12:9)

SHINE

Are you facing a situation today that is beyond you? A situation beyond your strength and your abilities that has you weary? Cry out to the One who is the Lord of Hosts, strong and mighty! Just speak your burden to Him. Spend time reflecting on the verses from today and on the fact that God is faithful beyond comprehension!

Day 49 — Alpha and Omega, Praise Him!

Let everything that has breath praise the LORD! Praise the LORD!
—Psalm 150:6

SOAK

We are called to continually praise the Lord. Everything that has breath is to praise the Lord. A wonderful way to rehearse who God is and what He has done is by rehearsing His character and attributes, and praying those back to the Lord in praise. We find evidence of God's character and ways throughout the Scriptures. I find it a helpful practice to make a note in my Bible or journal each time I run across a word or phrase that mentions a name of God or describes who He is or what He has done. Praise Him as Alpha and Omega, the beginning and the end!

Praise the LORD! Praise God in his sanctuary; praise him in his mighty heavens! Praise him for his mighty deeds; praise him according to his excellent greatness! Praise him with trumpet sound; praise him with lute and harp! Praise him with tambourine and dance; praise him with strings and pipe! Praise him with sounding cymbals; praise him with loud clashing cymbals! Let everything that has breath praise the LORD! Praise the LORD!
—Psalm 150:1-6

SHINE

A great exercise for personal prayer time, family devotions or with a small group is to praise God from A to Z. Just grab a sheet of paper and list the letters of the alphabet, A-Z. Then list an attribute, characteristic, or name of God for each one. Use this list to praise God today.

ABOUT THE AUTHOR

Susan is a writer, blogger, and speaker with a love and passion for God's Word. She has been teaching Bible studies to women for over 20 years. She currently serves on staff at her church. She and her husband, Chris, reside in Georgia. They have three grown children and five grandchildren. In her free time, Susan enjoys reading, baking, and spending time in her garden.

Follow Susan on her blog, https://susancady.com.

Made in the USA
San Bernardino, CA
18 June 2018